Hold the Line

Practical Guidance and Assignments in Written and
Oral Communication

John Pearce
Alan Cooper
Peter Leggott
Cyril Sprenger

Edward Arnold

© John Pearce, Alan Cooper, Peter Leggott
and Cyril Sprenger 1979

First published 1979
by Edward Arnold (Publishers) Ltd
41, Bedford Square, London WC1B 3DQ

Reprinted 1981

British Library Cataloguing in Publication Data
Hold the line.
  1. English language – Composition and exercises
  I. Pearce, John, *b.1928*
  428   PE1112

ISBN 0-7131-0358-2

Text set in 11/13pt VIP Plantin,
printed and bound in Great Britain at
The Pitman Press, Bath

Contents

Preface	v
Acknowledgements	vi
Notes for the teacher	vii

1	Communication	1
1.1	The essentials of communication	1
1.2	Conventions	1
1.3	Formality	2
1.4	Face-to-face	3
1.5	Status and role	7
1.6	Oral settings	8
1.7	Reading	9
1.8	Sources of information	11

2	Writing at work – letters and memoranda	15
2.1	Letter format	15
2.2	Letter styles	18
2.3	The setting	20
2.4	Personal letters	21
2.5	Business letters	21
2.6	Formal personal letters	23
2.7	Examples	23
2.8	Memoranda	26

3	Writing at work – notes and reports	28
3.1	Notes	28
3.2	Reports	30
3.3	Types of report	31
3.4	Report format	32
3.5	Reporting style	32
3.6	Reported form	34

4	Writing at work	37
4.1	Notices, announcements and circulars	37
4.2	The setting	38
4.3	Notice and instructions	39
4.4	Meetings	42
4.5	Circulars, forms and questionnaires	43
4.6	Pictorial representation	46

5	Words	52
5.1	The patterning of words	52
5.2	Assembled words	54
5.3	Organising meanings	55
5.4	Meaning and word order	57
5.5	The one, the self, and the many	58
5.6	Spelling	61

6	Punctuation	66
6.1	Why is punctuation a problem?	66
6.2	Punctuation and pauses	67
6.3	Punctuation as a separating system	67
6.4	The sentence stops	68
6.5	Stops as messages	69
6.6	The colon	70
6.7	The semi-colon	71
6.8	'Included units'	71
6.9	Specific meaning marks	74

7	The Assignment Approach	77
7.1	Language in real life	77
7.2	The Assignments	78
7.3	Worked Examples	78

The assignments

1. Millar's Motors	83
A Understanding the picture	84
B Len Forsyth	85
C Episodes on the Forecourt	85
D New recruit	86
2. Hunter Coaches Ltd	88
A Understanding the picture	89
B Coach Bookings	89
C Valley Forge Tours	90
D Managing the office	92
3. Riddles Ltd	94
A Understanding the picture	95
B Mrs Shaw's weakness	95
C The Bus Strike	96
D Office routines and problems	97
4. Mail Order	100
A Understanding the picture	101
B The executive assistant	101
C Setting up an office	102
D Setting up shop	103
5. Family in Action	105
A Understanding the picture	106
B Housing for Staff Nurse Charnwood	106
C South Nock Viaduct	108
D Road Safety	109
E Don't Knock the Rock	110
6. Butley Housing Department	112
A The old people's gardens	113
B The telephone message	113
C Demolition area	114
D The meeting arrangements	114
E Councillor Hunt's constituent	115
F The Housing Conference	116

Preface

This book has been written as a text book for students of English and communication skills. It is designed for those coming to courses in which English or communications is a compulsory element, but who do not have a qualification in English above Grade 3 of the CSE examination. The same authors have written *People in Touch* for students on courses at BEC National Level, and this one is intended as a companion volume for courses at or about BEC General Level.

Much of the work of this book is based on realistic situations drawn from real life. All of them are based on actual events in real places, but the names, both of people and places, many of the details and much of the order of events have been changed to make their original unrecognisable. Any direct resemblance to people or places or events which appears to remain in the text is unintentional.

The structure of the book provides a Manual and a set of Assignments. In the Manual there is a series of Activities designed to improve skills in specific aspects of oral and written communication. These Activities are related in each chapter to a particular theme or sphere of work, and serve to illustrate the chapter by concrete examples. While we believe firmly in the freedom of the teacher to choose material according to the needs of his class, we should stress that many of the tasks set in the Assignments later in the book will prove difficult for the student if he has not completed substantial work on the Activities in the first part of the book.

Most of the courses for which the students using this book will be working will have a clear set of learning objectives, but some of them cannot be provided for by a text book. One example is oral communication at a reception desk; another would be conversation on the telephone. The nearest approach made to this work in this book lies in the discussion tasks: teacher and students should not suppose these to be casual or unimportant. For other aspects of communication, and oral work in particular, it is intended that the teacher provide work which suits the class and its situation.

JJP
AC
PL
CS

Acknowledgements

We are indebted to numerous sources in business and academic fields for material and guidance. The section on spelling (5.6) is a free adaptation of a paper by J. D. Mountford (La Sainte Union College of HE, Southampton): *Spelling Junctions in English*, Proceedings of 4th International Congress of AILA, (Hochschul Verlag, 1977). The treatment of punctuation draws eclectically on Quirk *et al* – *Grammar of Contemporary English* (Longman 1976) and owes much to the work of David Brazil (Birmingham University) and Sylvia Warham (St Ives, Cambs.), but our use of their insights is our own responsibility. We have sought to ensure that our advice on presentation of letters etc is not in conflict with the rulings of the Royal Society of Arts, whose *Notes for Teachers and Candidates in Typewriting* rightly carry great weight. We are indebted to W. H. Coleman (Cambridge) for guidance in preparing the section on Pictorial Representation (4.6).

We are grateful to many teachers and colleagues who have encouraged us to develop the approaches used in *People in Touch* for National Level work so as to be of assistance to students at General Level. Sylvia Griffiths (Fielden Park CFE) and John Bowman (Derby CFE) have commmented valuably on drafts of the MS. All four of us can identify errors which would remain but for the vigilance of our wives. Jan Cutts typed the MS with professional interest as well as skill. Norma Anderson (Cambridgeshire LEA) greatly helped to improve early drafts, and Elli Ball (Huntingdon Technical College) read the final MS with a care which brought the text many benefits. It is not customary to acknowledge the work of one's editor, but the contribution Mike Rigby has made to both our books more than justifies an exception. Any faults which remain, however, are the authors' responsibility.

The publishers wish to thank I.C.I. Ltd., West Midlands County Council, the British Standards Institution and Shell U.K. Ltd. for permission to reproduce copyright material. (Page 46.)

Notes for the teacher

This book has been written for use in a wide range of courses and classes, and it is not possible to legislate for all of them. However, it is not designed to lessen the importance of the teacher. On the contrary, it requires decisions from the teacher at every step. These decisions need to be taken in the light of the teacher's assessment of his class and, particularly, the changes that occur as the students gain more skill. Such decisions will be about such matters as:

1. **Choice of material.** The material provided in the book is not designed to be worked through solidly by every class, even if the amount of time available were to allow this. Classes vary very much, but a representative BEC General Level group might well need to study between half and two thirds of the material in Chapters 1–6 and carry out between thirty and forty Activities before going on to a suitable selection of Assignments.

2. **Ordering of material.** The example given in the preceding paragraph assumes that the work on skills and Activities should come before Assignments. This may well be the case with only a minority of users: many teachers will wish to start with some Assignments, partly to find out which parts of the skills chapters are most needed. In that case, teachers and students alike should realise that Assignment methods take time to get used to, and the first assignment may take three or four times as long as later ones.

3. **Classroom approach.** The material in this book is not uniform in kind. Some sections, eg Chapter 2, could be used as students' private study or homework material, but other parts, such as Chapters 5 and 6, are designed to serve as a base for teaching and exposition and discussion in the classroom. We have assumed throughout that teachers will wish to make their own decisions about approach.

4. **Classroom methods.** Many of the Activities and most of the Assignment tasks are given focus by the use of an instruction term such as **Write** or **Draft**. In most cases this is self-explanatory, but many of these terms require a further decision from the teacher. Thus 'Write' leaves unresolved whether the students are to produce rough drafts, longhand fair copy, or clean typescript. More important, perhaps, 'Discuss' leaves open whether the discussion is in small groups, or in pairs, or among the class as a whole.

5. **Comprehension.** This book deals with comprehension on the basis of two principles: the detailed exploration of meanings is best done as an oral activity in class, and the best way of testing in writing whether the student understands his material is to give him tasks which make that understanding prerequisite. The absence of conventional comprehension exercises is intended to prevent the time-wasting use of written comprehension questions and answers. But the first assignment in each group is a careful test of inferential

comprehension and many of the Activities in Chapters 1–6 require very close attention to the meanings of words.

6. **Assessment.** We have not provided a detailed breakdown of the links between Assignments and the BEC learning objectives for Module 1 at General Level. Partly this is because many other courses are being catered for as well as BEC, partly it reflects the awkward fact that teachers can make given Tasks serve several different objectives according to the way they treat them. The use of material from this book for Assessed Assignments may not be acceptable to the BEC Moderator, and its use in duplicated form for class or test purposes requires the prior permission of the publisher. The teacher has to make local decisions about what assessment purposes are served by the use of particular Activities or Assignments.

The material about language in this book is written for use with native speakers of British English. There are many variations in conventions and styles about written communication which are peculiar to the language communities in which they exist. In the case of English, which exists in many varied forms all over the world, it may be unwise to assume that the instructions and rulings about correct usage given in this book will apply in other parts of the world. It is also unwise to assume that this book is designed for advanced language learning by students of English as a foreign language. They may find some of its material valuable as a guide to current practice in administration and business in Britain, but the learning activities and tasks are not designed to meet their needs.

1 Communication

1.1 The essentials of communication

We are four authors of a book, addressing a number of readers, whom we will usually address as 'you', the students who will use the book. To address you successfully, i.e. to communicate with you, we need to do three things:

1. know what kind of people we are addressing, our *audience*
2. understand the needs and skills of that audience, i.e. to match your *context*
3. make clear what we want to say, our *message*

A message may be a telegram, a letter or a whole book. The sender is placed in a setting of his own. He is addressing an audience which is in a context of its own. Adapting the message to suit the audience can happen naturally, as in writing a personal letter to a friend. In the course of this book we hope you will learn to do it as easily in a business setting.

1.1.1 Audience

We use the term *audience* to mean anyone who hears or reads a message, however long or short. Audiences differ more than might be supposed. Some audiences might not understand this use of the word audience at all: they would associate the word solely with a theatre or cinema. Some audiences would not be able to read a book at all, because they are not literate. Audiences might also be complicated: you form the student audience for this book, but your teachers form another audience of some importance.

1.1.2 Audience and context

Audiences vary, particularly those who read or use a book. You will vary in your previous experience of English teaching, your attitudes to your skills, in your beliefs about the value of the teaching you have had. We have to make some assumptions about these things. We have to assume, for example, that you can read reasonably well. We also assume that you are not as good at written English as you might like to be. But there are many other possible assumptions we do not make. For example, we do not assume that you have been taught English in any particular way. We have thought about these assumptions concerning our audience, and we shall ask you many times in using this book to do the same. You can also make some assumptions about us, of course. We hope that one of them will be this: we are not going to deceive you about the world of business and its requirements.

1.2 Conventions

Consider again a phrase from the previous paragraph, 'we are not going to deceive you about the world of business and its requirements'. We could have written, 'we aren't trying to con you about its demands'. That is a direct way of putting it, but 'con' would be a strange word to some readers and might not be found in some dictionaries. This kind of usage is often described as slang, and is treated by teachers as forbidden. Any advertiser will tell you, and will show you in his copywriting, that there is nothing forbidden about slang whatever: it is much too useful. The point is that it does not fit in a setting of business English because that English has to be explicit, and formal, but also human. That set of requirements – explicitness, formality and humanity – will run right through this book.

1.3 Formality

The underlying notion in the word 'deceive' is broadly the same as that in 'con', and very close to that in the colloquial phrase 'have you on'. These three ways of expressing the same basic idea correspond well to three levels in the formality with which ideas are expressed in English:

A	B	C
Deceive	con	have you on
Control oneself	keep calm	keep one's cool
Assess	size up	suss out
Satirize	poke fun at	take the mickey out of
You're wasting your time	get lost	get knotted

Column A shows the usage acceptable in a formal and explicit setting. Column C, which we may call Casual Usage, is perfectly acceptable usage in informal conversation both with friends and with many working colleagues. Column B is the battleground: opinions will vary, and people are entitled to different opinions, about how 'correct' these uses of language are. In general, do not be surprised if your teachers advise against using them in formal writing, but do not forget their value in softening the tone of otherwise rather chilly business letters.

Activity 1

Work out in discussion in pairs a set of five more phrases or words which would belong in the Casual column, and work out the versions which would fit in the other columns.

1.3.1 Levels of formality

The three levels of usage in the columns given in the previous paragraph can be described respectively as Formal, Consultative and Casual. Most business English writing is formal in style, but almost all business conversation is consultative in style. Conversation, both at business and away from work, between people who know one another well will almost always be casual in style. The term 'casual' should not be taken to imply any kind of disapproval. The same holds for 'consultative', which is a very valuable element in addressing people from an official standpoint: here is an example.

A

```
Madam,

I am instructed to request your attendance at
the Audiometry Clinic, Walker Park Hospital,
Corfield, at 13.30 hrs on Tuesday, March 9th.
You are required to bring with you any hearing
aids previously issued, whether in working order
or not.  Should you have any infection of the
ear, nose or throat or any communicable disease
you should notify the appointments clerk of your
inability to attend.

                           Outpatients (Audiometry)
                           Department.
```

B

Dear Mrs. Hutton,

Your doctor has referred you to us for hearing tests and we would like you to attend at the Audiometry Clinic, Walker Park Hospital, Corfield, at 13.30 hrs on Tuesday, March 9th. If you have previously had a hearing aid, please bring it with you, even if you do not use it at the moment. We prefer patients who have colds, coughs or other diseases to ring up and make another appointment.

            Yours sincerely,

            Outpatients Appointments
            Clerk.

The first version is perfectly correct, but is so formal that it sounds forbidding, and the last sentence could be difficult for some readers to grasp.

Activity 2

Make a list, in two columns, of at least twelve differences of expression between A and B.

1.3.2 Formality and explicitness

Being relatively formal and being explicit are related aspects of language. Consider the plumber who has sent his mate to collect some parts, and receives a telephone call from the storeman to clear up an uncertainty. At one point the exchange goes like this:

'D'you want self-locking?'
'Yes. You know the quantities?'
'Aye. But old or new?'
'New.'

The same instructions given in writing have to be quite explicit about these details:

'Please supply 1½ doz. 20 mm self-locking polythene-washered bi-metallic nuts.'

The wide application of this principle can be seen in the next section and in many of the Assignments later in the book.

1.4 Face-to-face

1.4.1 *Personal contact*

Contact between working colleagues or with members of the public occurs in thousands of situations. People come to enquiry counters to ask questions, to reception desks to seek information, to employment offices to seek jobs. These human contacts are often very brief, and in many offices the job of dealing with them is given to a very junior employee. How they are managed can make a great deal of difference to both the reputation of the office and the career of the young employee. There are at least five aspects to managing these situations, which we will deal with in turn: presenting the self, active participation, the rules of naming, conversational exchange, and accent.

1.4.2 *Presenting the self*

This is not mainly a question of 'selling' yourself at all. Here are some general guidelines which will build up a picture of how to do it:

1. Whenever a contact occurs for the first time, make sure that there is *eye contact* between you and the stranger, especially when you have asked a question.
2. Your own 'body language' has a strong effect on the nature of these contacts. Standing or leaning too close is one aspect of the matter; avoiding eye contact is another; wearing sunglasses indoors will disturb many enquirers; smoking or chewing gum in the presence of a

stranger is almost always felt to be rude, and in retail trade is sometimes grounds for dismissal; the classic signal of an attitude 'I don't care' is having one's feet on the desk.

3. Personal hygiene, and in particular the cleanliness and good odour of person and clothing, are basic good manners at work in all kinds of offices. It is generally regarded as offensive to comb the hair or clean the nails in public.

4. All employers have explicit or unwritten rules about dress, and it is unwise to challenge them until you are an established employee.

Activity 3

Explore in class discussion any points made by superiors at work or at school about your own self-presentation, and consider how far they were reasonable.

1.4.3 Active participation

All occasional contact, especially with strangers, places the officer or the employee of a public department or company in a position of needing to go half way to meet the needs of the stranger. A good example of the outlook is a notice in a Citizens' Advice Bureau in South London:

```
Disabled enquirers are asked to wait at the
yellow table, where a member of staff will
come to them.  Do not try to stand at the
main counter.
```

Another example occurred in an Education Office, and is given in two different versions:

A   'I want to ask about a grant.'
    'Yes, Madam. Who for?'
    'My boy.'
    'What does he need the grant for, Madam?'
    'Going back to college.'
    'Was he at university?'
    'Well, it's a bit private like and I'd rather not discuss it in public like this.'

B   'I want to ask about a grant.'
    'Yes, Madam. Would the grant be for you, Madam?'
    'No, not really; it's for my son.'
    'To help in his education?'
    'That's right.'
    'I see. What age is he, then?'
    '22. Coming up 23.'
    'He's in college, is he?'
    'Well, no. He wants to go back to college.'
    'Has he been in college?'
    'Oh yes. He was a brilliant student.'
    'Where was he?'
    'Loughborough. He was doing Physical Education . . . You know, training to be a teacher.'
    'When did he leave college?'
    'After his first year. Broke his legs in an accident mountaineering. Took two years to get over it.'
    'In that case, Madam, could I ask – if you don't mind my asking – why he's not making this enquiry for himself? I mean, most students do ask for themselves.'
    'Oh. He's still abroad. We're trying to get him to go back to college but he says he wouldn't get his grant.'

In A, the receptionist has to refer the enquiry to a colleague without knowing which one to select: the department has different assistants to deal with free school meals, school uniform, sixth-form maintenance grants, college awards, school bus passes, and higher education awards. The receptionist in B has picked her way much more carefully in asking one step at a time which leads her eventually to know exactly which colleague should be called in. There is much more to interviews than the words spoken, of course, but close study of these two examples is revealing of a number of important characteristics.

1.4.4 Special problems

Many enquirers arrive at a reception desk only because they have been driven there by annoyance or frustration. A man who complains angrily that his gas supply has been cut off without warning, for example, is entitled to be cross if the cut-out is unjustified. The receptionist's first task is to allow such anger to blow itself out without being ruffled oneself. Annoyance of this sort is very rarely directed at receptionists personally, and coping with it is one of the things they are paid for.

Special problems arise with enquirers who have one of a number of specific disabilities, and they arise much more commonly than most young employees anticipate. While blind people are easy to identify, they are also easy to underestimate. The partially-sighted, who usually cannot see to read, are at least three times more numerous than the blind, and may need a great deal of help, e.g. in completing forms and being shown exactly where to put the pen for signature. Deaf people may also be hard to identify if they do not have an obvious hearing aid. When you know you are speaking to a deaf person, be careful to let your mouth be clearly visible, and take care not to seem as though you think the deaf person a fool. This is much more difficult than it may seem.

1.4.5 Knowing what is wanted

Most employees work in the provision of goods or services which belong in specific ranges of types. Most approaches to receptionists, like those to shop assistants, come from enquirers who want one particular item without realising how large is the range of types from which it comes. The lady seeking the grant is a case in point: she has no reason to suppose that there are so many different kinds of grant. Goods identified in a catalogue can only be sold by assistants who can cope with multiple detail: shoes have variations in size, fitting, colour, style number, manufacturer and so forth; screws come in a score of combinations of gauge and length but in three or four finishes and several types of head; garments vary much as do shoes. In face-to-face contact, establishing the customer's precise requirements means asking a series of questions without making the customer feel a fool, and without being in any way pressing.

Activity 4

For this activity, work in pairs, one taking the part of an assistant in a shop selling clothes or shoes or hardware, the other taking the part of a customer. The customer has a specifc purchase in mind, shows the assistant a card reading as follows:

> I AM A DEAF MUTE, AND CANNOT HEAR OR SPEAK.
> ARE YOU WILLING TO HELP ME THROUGH WRITING NOTES ON MY PAD?

Conduct the exchange which follows.

Activity 5

Members of the class should take it in turn to play the part of a traffic warden or policeman. Each one who does so is given a particular spot in the town he knows well, and another member of the class comes up to him and asks for directions to another point in the town. The questioner adds, 'I am partially sighted and can't read street names.'

1.4.6 Naming

Every language has rules of personal address which reflect social relationships. The rules of what people call each other by name in Britain are rather confused. Work relationships used to be governed solely by status: some addressed any superior as 'Sir' or 'Madam', or by Title + Surname; one addressed any male junior by surname only, and any female junior by first name. This pattern still survives, but is steadily giving way to several continuing changes:

1. In all kinds of organisation, senior staff now generally call each other by first-name. If you are addressed so by an equal, do the same in return – but be sure he *is* an equal. If addressed by first name by a superior, wait until invited to use first name in reply, and not even then in a formal setting such as a meeting.
2. The spread of first-name usage has led some to use it to force the social pace, to make relationships feel closer than in reality they are. This leaves everyone with much greater control over the matter than used to be the case: we all have the two weapons of insisting on title + surname to a person who first-names us, and if we want to be really rude, the use of surname only.
3. Although first-names are widely used, often people in senior positions or particular jobs make their own rules. Other people, too, retain conventional usage. For example, clergy are still properly addressed as 'Vicar' or 'Father' in conversation, where the usage 'Reverend' is incorrect. Heads of schools are often addressed as 'Head Master' or 'Head Mistress' in formal sessions such as meetings of governors, but for a teaching staff to tolerate this for routine exchanges is very rare. There are special naming rules in the Armed Forces and the Courts of Law, but no layman will suffer from not knowing them.

Activity 6

Explore in discussion the naming practices of your previous school, places of work you have known, and places where naming may be unusual – e.g. the Armed Forces or hairdressing salons.

1.4.7 Conversational exchange

People in conversation take turns. This apparently simple and very obvious fact hides some not so obvious points. In order to take a turn in the conversation, you have to know that the other person has finished his turn. You have to recognise how the other person can 'throw the ball to you'. In taking your turn, you complete it with the same sort of signal to the person you are talking to. We all of us take these facts about conversation completely for granted, but they are worth a little study.

Activity 7

For this activity, a number of pairs of students are to study in detail version B of the conversation given in paragraph 1.4.3 above.

Each pair should be asked to repeat the conversation out loud in *one* of the following ways:

1. in the ordinary way with both participants taking a sensible part in conversation and understanding one another well.
2. with the enquirer never quite waiting for the receptionist to finish her questions and appearing constantly to interrupt.
3. the receptionist failing to understand either when the enquirer had not finished or the need to allow her to do so, and constantly hurrying on with the next question.

Discuss what precisely the difficulties in each of the three conversations have been.

1.4.8 Taking Turns

The role of turn-taking in conversation is peculiar in the case of enquiry counters for two reasons. One is that just as every individual has his own accent and way of speaking, so he may have his own way of signalling his conversational turn-taking. These individual qualities of speech have to be listened to by the receptionist every time. Some experts believe that this careful listening for qualities of speech is the main activity going on when people are 'talking about the weather'. Unfortunately enquirers at counters do not talk about the weather, so receptionists need to be people with a very quick ear for speech. They do not get much time to 'tune in'. This skill is in fact much easier to learn than might be supposed, particularly from mixing with a wide variety of social groups or from travelling about the country.

The other peculiarity about enquiry desk conversations is that the enquirer often expects the receptionist to make the running, sometimes expecting the receptionist to understand the question before it has been put. Receptionists need to be very sensitive to the degree of initiative expected of them, and to be ready to take the lead in such contacts if that will help the business forward.

1.4.9 Speech patterns

The final aspect of face-to-face contact is speech accent. Many enquirers are shy of reception desks, for fear the receptionist will be 'well spoken', and make them embarrassed about their own speech. In some cases a receptionist may be able to move her own accent clearly towards that of the enquirer, and this is a skill which is to be greatly encouraged. There need be nothing artificial about moving towards the accent of the person you are talking to. This pattern is known as *convergence*, and it is a well-established and very common fact of life.

1.5 Status and role

Every personal encounter is also likely to be affected by what the participants in it regard as their relative status. This refers to one of two ways in which people sort themselves out from the mass. One is *social* status: the lady coming to the counter to ask about a grant may be expensively dressed, carefully groomed, and 'posh' in speech, and all these things project an impression of her standing. But the absence of them may also convey an impression of it, and the same holds for the receptionist. This complex business of social status is usually labelled 'class', and speech and dress and manners all enter into it, but it is far more complicated than occupation.

1.5.1 Job status

Quite different from social status is *job* status. That may be formal status, based on an employee's rank or salary or both. Or it may be informal status, based on a reputation for skill or wisdom or human quality. A great many organisations depend for their smooth running on a pleasant relationship between the boss or head of department, who has the highest formal status, and someone in the staff who may not be at all senior but is the informal leader or spokesman for the employees because he has the highest informal status.

1.5.2 Role

Any employee in contact with someone from outside his own organisation is representing it. He is not entirely free to speak or write as a private individual: that is, he has a role or function which is not that of his private life. This is true of every employee in principle. You will sometimes see 'role' in this context identified with playing a role or part in a theatre, but the image is misleading: our roles as employees for the most part come naturally and are best played without pretence or artificiality. There are numerous instances of individuals being asked to adopt employee roles in the Assignments later in this book.

1.6 Oral settings

The oral aspects of English which are likely to face you in early years of work have to do with receiving instructions, transmitting messages, asking and answering questions on the telephone and (more often than you might expect) reading aloud or dictating material.

1.6.1 Reading aloud

This is a more valuable skill than it may seem and a more difficult task than many suppose. You are likely to be asked to do it several times during your course and the guidelines to observe as far as possible are these:

1. prepare the reading by studying the text in detail.
2. make your reading as near to ordinary fluent speech as you can make it.
3. adjust the pace of your reading to the needs of your audience, especially by making pauses or repetitions if they are making notes.

Activity 8

The class should work in groups of four or five. Each group should select four pieces for reading aloud, prepare the readings, and present them orally to the class. Any one group should aim at a maximum of 4–4½ minutes' reading. The pieces should include:

1. a news item from a current newspaper's sport pages.
2. a story written for very young children.
3. a slightly complicated announcement for reading over the PA system of a station or airport.
4. a mock news item of the kind used in a 'Next Week's News' satire.

Discussion should focus on the different styles of reading required by the different texts.

1.6.2 Telephone contact

You cannot see or be seen when talking by telephone. A stranger may need to hear your name twice, will need time to get used to your voice or accent, will be entitled to know who you are and why you wish to speak to him. Any means of establishing a link will help and a clear statement of your business is vital. Note the following guidelines:

1. The telephone is a microphone, best used a

full inch or more from the mouth.

2. Do not 'bark' your name or office in answering a call, and try to avoid having three-quarters of your response to a call lost in the fact that the bell is still ringing.

3. Taking messages on the telephone calls for a set of rough notes which are written up afterwards, and every message must:

a. identify the caller by name and telephone number.
b. give the date and time of the message.
c. give the content of the message clearly.

4. It is a good rule, and in some offices it is insisted on, that the telephone enquirer should not be told whether the person he seeks is in until the caller has identified himself.

5. A telephone left 'off the hook' while you seek the person called is very expensive.

The commonest defects in message taking are:

a. omitting a digit from a long telephone number;
b. omitting to ask the caller who or what he is other than his name;
c. failing to get the caller's telephone number at all. The best way to prevent these errors is to make it a fixed rule to read the message back to the caller in 'memorandum format' (see 2.8).

1.7 Reading

If you are on a course using this text book, obviously you can read. One vital question, however, is not whether you can read, but how well. Reading well does not mean reading quickly: there are good fast readers and good slow readers Reading well means four things:

1. Extracting the meaning from the text.
2. Relating it to what you already know.
3. Assessing the material for its accuracy, honesty or relevance to your purpose.
4. Doing all three things without wasting time or effort on the task.

1.7.1 How not to do it

Let us begin with two examples. Suppose you want to find out whether you can go by train from Stevenage to Ely, and obtain the National BR time-table book. Do you flip through the 1,200 pages looking for the two towns in the headings? If so, you would find Ely on the Norwich–Peterborough line and Stevenage on the London–Newcastle one, which connect only at Peterborough. Taking that route, your journey could take five hours. If you used the index at the front, you would find a link from Stevenage to Cambridge and then on to Ely, which can usually be done in about half as long.

Secondly, suppose you want to know how paraffin is made. A library list might refer you to oil refining, and if you are an inefficient reader you might well spend two hours reading a whole book, whereas an efficient one would use the index at the back, scan two pages, and find the five lines he wants in five minutes.

1.7.2 Reading skills

Inefficient and laboured reading can rapidly demoralise you. Many of you will know this from experience, although you may not have realised at the time that it was your limited reading skills that were making school so depressing. Do not fall into the trap of supposing that skill in reading simply means reading faster, or that reading faster is necessarily more efficient. It may be, but equally it may just increase the pace at which you waste time on unproductive reading. Being an efficient reader means being able to vary your approach to what you are reading, and vary your reading technique to match the purposes you have in mind. Reading skills can be learned, even quite late in life, and if you find your Course text books difficult to read, you should set out to improve your skills.

1.7.3 A plan for improving your reading

1. Find reading material which you read fairly easily, and which you enjoy, and read a great deal of it. The vast majority of people whose reading skills need further development are behind-hand simply because they have not read enough. Paperback fiction, science fiction, a weekly magazine – anything which is in continuous writing will serve. Try to read for a substantial stretch of time (i.e. at least an hour at a time). This reading should be attentive, not the reading equivalent of background music. After three novels, or the equivalent, step up the level a shade to books a little more 'serious' – still novels, or comment weeklies, or the 'posh' Sundays, and keep up the quantity regularly. When you find an author you like, read other books by the same writer: one of the signs of a 'growing' reader is a phase of staying with one author. A clear sign of a reader who is growing beyond a particular writer is that he gets bored with him.
2. Sometimes it is necessary to obtain the main ideas from a passage. In this case all you need do is to read straight through it, concentrating on the most important parts. This is what you do when you read novels or magazine articles. Sometimes, however, you may need to work out the inner meaning of what is written; there may be complicated sequences of meaning to unravel, or a complex argument to follow. In such a case, expect to read much more slowly. Expect to pause quite often, reading some parts more than once. Expect to make a mental review every so often of what you have understood up to that point, or even to make some notes. Even the most skilled readers sometimes need to do these things, and doing them is not a sign of inefficient reading. Pausing and reflecting can help everyone to grasp and remember difficult ideas.
3. When you have to read information material, such as textbooks or reference books, practise the methods of the skilled reader:

a. headline hopping or moving quickly through the pages and down each page to find the particular parts you need;
b. scanning, or making a slow glance through the essentials of a page or a chapter to find out whether it contains what you are seeking;
c. skimming, or going through a chapter where you want some parts but not others, without wasting time on the parts you do not need.

Scanning and skimming are sometimes thought of as improper things to do. Almost all adult readers, however, do a certain amount of skimming, and all efficient readers do a great deal of scanning. A teacher looking for a section on, say, alphabetical order in this book would be very inefficient if he were to read solemnly through the whole text instead of glancing through section headings and paragraph titles which we have so carefully provided. However, scanning and skimming will give you very little that you can retain unless you note it down.
4. A further important reading skill is that of evaluating what you read, deciding whether something is fact or opinion, whether an argument is logical or not, or whether bias or propaganda is pretending to be straight fact. When you have this kind of material to read, it is important not to jump to conclusions, not to be led by first impressions. Advertisements, circulars and direct-mail sales material are often so cleverly written that they deceive. Try reading some of these very closely: a skilled reader is a critical reader, and does not automatically accept what he reads because it is in

black and white, but matches it against his own experience and goes on thinking about it afterwards.

5. Sooner or later, in college or at work, you are likely to need the skill of reading aloud. This is a useful asset for anybody, but is also a more useful job-skill than is usually realised. Learning how to read aloud competently is also, for most people, a remarkably good way of improving their silent reading as well. Try using a cassette tape-recorder and read aloud into it for three or four minutes every day for a week, with another week a month later and a longer time for each reading. Play the recording back each time, and if you do not like the result, record the same text again. The improvement with each repeat recording is usually far greater than you will expect.

Activity 9

Using the help provided by the Contents page and the paragraph headings of this book, **list as rapidly as possible** the pages and paragraph numbers dealing with the five topics mentioned in paragraph 5 above.

1.8 Sources of information

One of the clearest differences between school and the world of work is that schools provide information in prepared form, while after school you are likely to have to go and seek it for yourself. In order to do this with any hope of success you need to know first what the possible sources are.

Activity 10

Visit the reference section of a library such as that in a college of further education or a branch of the public library. **Scan** the whole section and **select** six titles which appear of interest. **Study** these six volumes with attention to the kind of information given, how it is organised, and what is shown on the contents page. **Write notes** on the relative value of the six.

1.8.1 Using sources of information

Consider again the instructions given in the previous activity: *scan, select, study* and *write notes*. The most important single skill in using sources of information is not in fact that of reading the material when you have found it. Rather, it is the skill of finding it quickly. One element of this is the ability to use alphabetical order; another is the ability to go first to a contents page or index and scan it in order to see whether you are likely to find what you are looking for. A third element is the ability to *skim over* whole pages or chapters of a book to see whether the information you seek is given there or not.

1.8.2 Interpreting queries

The other important skill in seeking information is knowing where to go. Many young people suppose that they will lose face if they reveal that they do not know where to find information – for instance by asking a librarian. In a sense, the word 'librarian' is misleading: it gives an image of people who stamp books and put them back on shelves. In reality a librarian is a specialist in information: his most important job is to know where to go for material, especially technical or specialised material.

The ordinary employee, however, cannot leave all information-seeking to the librarian, especially as a good deal of the information needed in many businesses is what most adults would call 'general knowledge'. The kind of activity suggested in Activity 10 needs to be followed up by a closer study and use of a particular work of reference. The next exercise is an example.

Activity 11

You should suppose that you are assistant secretary of the sports club at the industrial firm where you work. You are suddenly burdened with additional work when the Secretary goes into hospital for a two-month stay just as a number of major functions are being planned. In the course of this work you have to make use of a wide range of reference books, and the specific tasks which lead you to do this are listed below. In each case, **identify where you would look** for the information needed, either to find it or to check the accuracy of what you already know. In some cases you will need to use more than one source, and merely to ask a librarian would evade the real task.

a. The five largest industrial employers within a ten-mile radius.
b. The name and address of the local elected county or metropolitan district councillor for your home area, and the same information for the chairman of that council.
c. The club owns some silver or silver-plate pieces; where do you look to find out whether the marks on them are hall-marks?
d. A boaster in the club bar has been on a trip round the world, and claims to have visited nineteen countries in going by road from Vancouver to Valparaiso. Where do you check his facts, and establish whether such a road journey is possible?
e. The club chairman has to attend a conference in Manchester for works club chairmen; but he is in Cambridge the previous day and cannot leave before noon. He wants to know what route to take by train and how many changes will be necessary.
f. The club has a choir which gives an annual concert. You are asked to draw up the basic facts for the programme – check the spelling of composers' names, give their dates, etc.
g. The committee have heard that the local education authority is desperate for playing field space for a nearby school while a new ground is seeded; who should you write to with an offer of help and how do you find the address?
h. The club's 50th Anniversary Dinner is in prospect, and former members who are now well known include an MP, a life peer, and a rear-admiral. How do you find out how to address them in a letter?
i. How do you find out the proper order in which the dinner should be organised (i.e. speakers, etc)?
j. How do you find out what constituency the MP represents and the size of his majority?
k. One of the prospective guests, it is hoped, will be a well-known comedian. How do you find out where and how to arrange this?
l. Before inviting the guests you have to be sure of hotel rooms for them. Where do you look to evaluate the possibilities?
m. The guests have to be notified rather late in the arrangements that the dinner has been moved from one hotel to another, and one of them can only be reached by international telephone. Where do you look for guidance on making such a call?
n. How do you find out, without going to a Post Office, whether the silver pieces mentioned in question c can be posted first class in one parcel or not?
o. Two of the guests at the dinner happen to be sons of very famous fathers (now dead). Where do you check the facts about the fathers?
p. The club chairman asks you to check how he should pronounce a series of half a dozen

long words – e.g. where to put the stress. What source should you use?

1.8.3 Specific sources

Some sources of information need particular study and attention, not so much in order to know what is in them but rather to know how to use them easily. These are the 'Yellow Pages', *Kelly's Directory*, the *Post Office Guide* and *Whitaker's Almanack*.

A. 'Yellow Pages' is the colloquial name for the *Classified Telephone Directory*. It includes the telephone numbers of all kinds of businesses and traders, classified under trade headings. It is not necessary to know the name of a firm to use it: a number of firms may appear under each heading. It is necessary, however, to know whether firms will be classified under 'Garages' or 'Motor Vehicle Agencies' or 'Car Servicing', and that requires some study of the directory.

Activity 12

Find out the classification in your local 'Yellow Pages' for firms which conduct the following kinds of business:

a. second-hand good-condition clothing shops
b. stone cleaning
c. repairing power-tools
d. sell furniture at a discount
e. provide clerical services in the customer's own home
f. repair damaged roof structures
g. re-point brickwork
h. re-seed tennis courts or fields
j. descale water systems.

B. *Kelly's Directory* comes in many forms, local as well as national. The principal form is the *Directory of Manufacturers and Merchants* (Volume 1 United Kingdom, Volume 2 International). The first volume covers the whole of the UK and is similar to the 'Yellow Pages' but gives Telex as well as telephone numbers.

Activity 13

Your club committee faces the need to re-equip the football side of the club with every item from goalposts and corner-flags to balls and line-marking equipment. You already have a British supplier but are instructed to obtain quotations from others. *Find the names and addresses* of possible suppliers, including at least three from EEC countries.

Activity 14

Carry out the same task for the supply of bar equipment.

C. *The Post Office Guide* is the most complete and informative treatment of postal services in the world. It repays careful study of its contents and organisation.

Activity 15

Suppose that three items of bar equipment have been ordered from a supplier in Takaoka, and have arrived in unusable condition. You need to convey this information to the supplier immediately. **Establish,** therefore, where Takaoka is, what it would cost to communicate by air mail, telephone, cable, etc., and what means would be available to you if the supplier's office hours do not coincide with your own.

D. *Whitaker's Almanack* is published annually and it may be important to use an up-to-date edition. It is the most comprehensive assembly available of all kinds of information, including sporting organisations, institutions and societies, trade and professional journals, and even annual reference books. It gives valuable guidance on etiquette and procedure, government, parliament, law, taxation and much else.

Activity 16

Devise an inquiry for a fellow-student which will require him or her to make use of *Whitaker* and at least one other reference book.

2
Writing at work – letters and memoranda

This chapter is about the most routine forms of written communication: letters and memoranda. It begins with some basic guidance about the layout and format of letters, with some examples, followed by an account of a situation in which the later examples and activities take place.

2.1 Letter Format

There are two main categories of letter: firm-to-firm, and person-to-firm. Letters from firm-to-person can be treated exactly like letters firm-to-firm. Nowadays, virtually all business correspondence is typed on headed paper, and each company has its own rules about the layout of its own correspondence. We shall be concerned, therefore, with letters in the person-to-firm category, with some attention to those going person-to-person.

The layout and presentation of business letters is important, because letters are ambassadors and advertisements for the firms which send them out. The same applies to letters sent in a business context by private individuals.

2.1.1 Principles of layout

The traditional format of the hand-written letter is shown in diagram A: it has a sloped format for the sender's address in the upper right hand part of the letter with the date

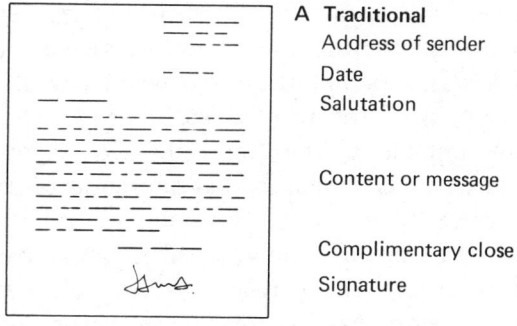

A **Traditional**
Address of sender
Date
Salutation

Content or message

Complimentary close
Signature

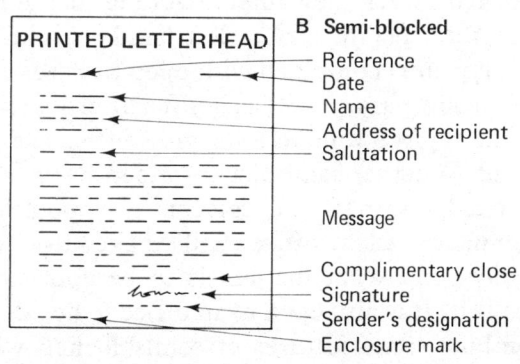

B **Semi-blocked**
Reference
Date
Name
Address of recipient
Salutation

Message

Complimentary close
Signature
Sender's designation
Enclosure mark

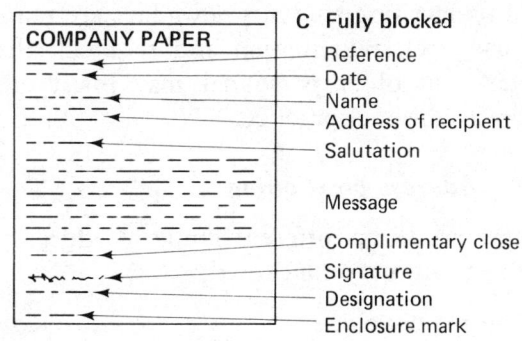

C **Fully blocked**
Reference
Date
Name
Address of recipient
Salutation

Message

Complimentary close
Signature
Designation
Enclosure mark

underneath it, indenting of each paragraph, and a signature towards the right. A handwritten letter will not usually have a recipient's address, but if such a letter is typed the address will be against the left hand margin, below the signature. This layout is virtually never used in a business context nowadays, because business letters use paper with a printed letter head. Some individuals may like to have their addresses printed for private use in a single line across the whole page, or in some other format: this is entirely a matter of individual choice. The earlier practice of business was to adopt the same layout, with the exception of the printed letter head. This is now known as the 'semi-blocked' arrangement, and is shown in diagrammatic form in diagram B.

The nature of typing, with the greater ease of returning the carriage to the left hand-margin-stop, has led to the use of the layout shown in diagram C, which is known as 'fully blocked'. Every new line, including that of the signature, begins on the left hand margin. If this layout is combined with open punctuation (see below para. 2.1.4) a significant proportion of the typist's time in a business office can be saved. Whether semi-blocked (as in B) or fully blocked (as in C) is 'correct' is a pointless argument: each office will make its own choice, and what matters is to be consistent about it. It is also open to an office to decide to combine some features of semi-blocked with some features of fully blocked. All shorthand and typewriting students nowadays are taught to use open punctuation and to block their letters but older personnel may insist on a more traditional practice.

2.1.2 Address positioning

There are three different kinds of address so far as position is concerned:

1. on the envelope
2. the address of the sender of the letter
3. the recipient's address if shown on the letter

a. *On an envelope* the address may be sloped or blocked, and if sloped is usually punctuated in full. For the punctuation of blocked layout see below. For layout see 2.2.1

b. The address of the sender, if it is not shown as a printed letter head, should appear in the upper right area of the paper (not the extreme corner). In a hand-written letter this address should be sloped with full punctuation. In a typewritten letter it may be either sloped with punctuation or blocked.

c. The address of the recipient, if it is shown, is always blocked (i.e. vertical) on the left hand margin,

(i) in business letters, above the opening.
(ii) in private letters on business matters, below the signature, if at all.
(iii) in personal letters, normally omitted.

2.1.3 Address format

Here are the three normal formats for writing addresses, whether on envelopes or letters:

1

```
J H R Williams & Sons
22 Parliament Street
Mapples Cross
DONNERSLEY
QN4 2BX
```

2

```
J. H. R. Williams & Sons,
22 Parliament Street,
Mapples Cross,
DONNERSLEY,
QN4 2BX
```

3

```
       J. H. R. Williams & Sons,
         22 Parliament Street,
            Mapples Cross,
               DONNERSLEY,
                  QN4 2BX
```

2.1.4 Address punctuation

If it is the custom of your employer or your teacher of typewriting to insist on open punctuation as in 1 above, there are very few circumstances in which any comma or full stop will be required in laying out an address. In other cases, the pattern to use is shown in examples 2 and 3 above. Note that it is not correct to place a comma between the house number and the street name. On the same principle, if a name of a person is written out in full (eg Helen Margaret Fowles) it is incorrect to place any stop after any forenames.

2.1.5 Post codes

No address in the UK is technically complete without a Post Code. The widespread belief that the Post Office does not in fact use its Post Codes is a myth. Post Codes should also *not* be underlined or punctuated, and should be given a line to themselves at the end of the address.

2.1.6 Overseas practice

Letter-layout varies considerably from country to country. In particular:

1. Many European addresses begin with the post code and city number and have the street name last thus:

```
         8000 MUNCHEN 22
         Ohmallee 12.
```

In such cases, a letter without the relevant codes is likely not to be delivered.

2. In North America the alternative to a post code is known as a 'Zip Code', a five-digit number which is essential in that letters without a zip code do not in the legal sense have to be delivered. Address layout is almost always blocked and in open punctuation. Thus, what is spoken as '14 22 North Fourteenth Street, Baltimore, Maryland 21213' will be typed thus:

```
1422 N 14

Baltimore

MD 21213

U S A
```

This address will be hand-written thus:

1422 N 14,
Baltimore,
Md, 21213,
U.S.A.

2.1.7 Names, initials and qualifications

The use of 'Esq.' has now largely disappeared, and its complete disappearance would be a very good thing. There are three generally acceptable presentations for personal names in addresses:

1. title, initial/forename, surname, thus:
Miss Helen Fowles; Miss H. M. Fowles; Ms H. M. Fowles; Messrs. Haldane & Gibson.

2. initial/forename, surname, one qualification, thus:
C. W. Fowles M.A.; George Carter OBE.
3. Quaker usage: first name and surname only, thus:
Helen Fowles; George Carter.

In any of these three uses, if you know a second initial it is courteous to use it. The use of more than one set of letters after the name is generally felt to be pretentious except in academic life, where it is acceptable to add an honour or distinction to the chosen single qualification, thus:

    C W Harper   O B E   M A

Attempts have been made to prescribe the order in which these should be placed, but practice varies. The practice of listing long strings of qualifications or honours after a name in a letter-head or a signature designation is undesirable and may easily be thought ridiculous.

Practice in these matters appears to be changing rapidly. Most published authorities rule firmly that a title or the use of Esq is obligatory, but social change, including for example the Women's Movement, has made for much more mixed customs. If you have a format in which you prefer to be addressed, use it in your own letter signatures, and it is a good rule to address others in the way in which they refer to themselves. A lady who leaves you in doubt between Miss or Mrs does not want you to use either.

2.2 Letter styles

English custom has a clear etiquette of naming and modes-of-address in face-to-face contact, and this extends to letters. While custom in face-to-face contact, as we have seen, has changed a great deal, it has changed little in letters. Here we can set out the conventions in a table:

Kind of contact	salutation (or 'top')	valediction (or 'tail')	style
1. Firm to firm	Dear Sirs	Yours faithfully	formal
2. Firm to firm's named officer	Dear Mrs X	Yours sincerely	formal
3. Firm to person (not met or known)	Dear Sir	Yours faithfully	formal
4. Person to firm	Dear Sirs	Yours faithfully	formal
5. Person to firm's named officer	Dear Mrs X	Yours sincerely	consultative
6. Person to unknown person	Dear Madam	Yours faithfully	formal
7. Person to known person	Dear Mrs X	Yours sincerely	consultative
8. Person to friend	Dear Tom	Yours	consultative/casual

Note: The use of Yours sincerely is reserved for letters where the recipient has been addressed by name.
In all cases, Yours F̲aithfully, and Yours S̲incerely and Your's are errors.
Some categories of public officers and almost all holders of titles, including peers, royalty, clergy, judges, mayors, Ministers and MP's should be addressed according to rules set out in *Whitaker's Almanack*, but if you cannot refer to this the forms Dear Sir or Dear Madam are always acceptable. In circular letters, it is better to leave out the salutation than to write Dear Sir/Madam. In all other letters, if you know the name, use it.

```
                                44A, Potter Lane  ─┐         ──── This comma wrong
                                Hanbury            │
                                New Fordage, ◄─────┤         ──── Blocked layout acceptable but hardly appropriate here
                                Lancs             ─┘         ──── Punctuation mixes up open and full
                                                             ──── Postcode missing

4th July, 1979 ◄─────────────────────────────────────────── Date format correct, others acceptable. Date position is
                                                                  better below the address in a personal letter.
Dear Sir, ◄──────────────────────────────────────────────── or Dear Archdeacon

Thank you for your kind invitation to attend
the Service of Thanksgiving on the occasion
of the 700th Anniversary of the Church of All
Saints, Golbury.   I am very pleased to be   ◄──────────── Spacings correct; indented text preferable
asked and would have liked to attend, but I                   in a personal letter
am recovering from a major operation.   I must
beg to be excused, and regret missing what
will, I am sure, prove an inspiring occasion.

            Yours faithfully, ◄─────────────────────────── This position for the complimentary close and signature
              Arthur Smith                                     is traditional, and is inconsistent with the use of
                                                               blocked layout in the address above
                                                          ──── Title of sender not needed since the invitation was
                                                               correctly addressed
The Very Rev W R Gray   ◄───────────────────────────────── Recipient's address, if shown at all in a personal
Archdeacon of Hanbury                                          letter, is correctly placed here and correctly blocked
The Vicarage                                              ──── 'Archdeacon of Hanbury' is superfluous: strictly, it is
Bridge Street                                                  an alternative to Mr Gray's name
Golbury
Lancs                                                     ──── Most recipients would regard a letter of this kind as
                                                               more personal and so more appropriate if it were
                                                               written by hand
```

```
                           From  ◄─────────────────────── 'from' here is always incorrect
                           201  Longston High Road  ─┐ ── Sender's address should observe consistent slope
                              Darlbury Green          │    with date vertically below last line of address.
                                 Darlbury             │    Open punctuation in sloped layout incorrect
Stowe  Burton & Cousinson       Nr Oldchester OL9 6TR │
Bank Chambers (2nd flr)              14. 2.79        ─┘ ── Recipient's address positioned too high: should
   Turnford Square  ◄───────────                           start below the date-line
      Oldchester 2                                     ── Date format acceptable but not ideal
                                                       ── Recipient's address on the LH margin should always
Dear Sirs, ◄─────────────────────────────────────────     be blocked
                                                       ── Salutation too close to address above
    Thank you for your letter informing me that you  ─┐
are now free to pay me the legacy left me by my sister.│
I would prefer to be paid by cheque and would like to  │◄── Message brief and clear
call, as you suggest, on December 19th at 11 a.m.     ─┘

        Your's sincerely, ◄──────────────────────────── 'Dear Sirs' requires Yours faithfully
           Mary Cadmans                                    Apostrophe wrong
        (Mrs) Mary Cadmans  ◄─────────                     Position of close acceptable

                                                       ── In a handwritten letter, use signature only, with
                                                          title in brackets *after* it if recipient does not
                                                          know it from previous correspondence
```

19

2.2.1 Envelopes

The address on an envelope should be set out, either in sloped or blocked layout, with the recipient's name half way down the envelope and the address in mid position across the envelope's width. An example is set out. Note that it is always incorrect to write 'To' on an envelope, or 'To/'.

```
              James Holloway Esq
              22 Coppindale Road
              CHELTENHAM
              Gloucestershire
              CH3 4LP
```

2.3 The setting

Helen Fowles is almost 21, and is studying for an HND in Catering and Hotel Management at Ledsham College of Technology. She had left school at the age of 16, with 4 O-Levels, and had found herself a job working in a local hotel. She was able to gain experience of most of the jobs which are done in the hotel trade, and in the course of two years became an Assistant to the General Manager. Rather to her surprise, she found the work fascinating and decided to qualify for it properly. She worked part time for A-Level, and gained a grant to pursue her HND Course.

An only child, Helen then lost her parents in an airline disaster just after her twentieth birthday. She inherited the family home in Windsor, but since she would not be able to live in it for at least three years she decided to sell it and buy one to live in Ledsham while she completed her course. She took advice from the solicitor who worked for the Students' Union at Ledsham College of Technology, visited a large number of houses, commissioned a survey on one which attracted her, and eventually made a successful offer to buy No. 16 Butter Lane, Ledsham. This is a six-roomed end-of-terrace house in a quiet road where many students have houses of the same sort. It has been occupied by an old lady who inherited it from her parents, the owners for whom the house was built in 1912. According to the surveyor's report it needs complete rewiring, complete new plumbing, a number of repairs to the roof, chimneys and guttering, and a thorough modernisation of the heating and hot water system. Her offer to buy the house is accepted and purchase is completed.

2.3.1

We shall see in the documents which arise in the experience of Helen's purchase of this house a number of examples of business writing, some good and some bad. There is a crucial difference between business writing which is formal and writing which struggles so hard to be correct that it fails to communicate. Helen herself had seen so much poor writing in the course of her work that she had learned a great deal about how to communicate efficiently. She typed out a list of forty-four jobs which needed to be done on 16 Butter Lane, obtained a list of suitable contractors from the surveyor, and sent all of them a copy of her list, asking them to submit estimates for whatever items on it they felt able to undertake. The items range from 'replace front door lock and fit security chain' to 'enlarge loft entry to take new cold system and make good'. She does not expect to be able to afford all the items, and wants separate sums quoted for each item so that she can make choices. She tells each of the contractors this fact in her covering letter. Some of the replies are given in Section 2.7, below, for discussion in the light of the intervening work.

2.4 Personal letters

Letters from one person to another need to take account of individual qualities and limitations. For example, Helen Fowles was buying a house with a telephone installed, and wanted to make sure that the people leaving the house did not ask the Post Office to take it out. However, the previous occupant, Mrs Gore, is a lady of 79 who has never done business herself, and is likely to be frightened by a typed letter, so Helen writes to the Post Office asking for the instrument to be left in and for the bills to be sent to her, but has to make sure that Mrs Gore does not issue contradictory instructions (*see right*):

Students who can type may wonder whether this sort of letter should be typewritten. The answer entails working out how the reader would react. Mrs Gore would probably find a typed letter disturbing. But attitudes among younger people are very different.

In all personal letters a sender's address remains essential, if only because the Post Office may have to return your letter; so does a date, in case you write again next day to the same reader, who may get muddled.

2.5 Business letters

The immense variety of business letters makes it difficult to lay down any general rules or guidelines. One set of examples has already been given, and others will follow. All of them suggest a simple general rule about the tone of business letters: be as direct and unstuffy as you can, without becoming chatty.

> Dear Mrs. Gore,
>
> It was so nice of you to see me and let me measure up for curtains. You have a lovely house and I am looking forward to living in it.
>
> Could I make a special request about the telephone. I have arranged with the Post Office for me to take it over, and I will be paying for it from the day you move out. Could you mention to your brothers that they do not need to tell the Post Office anything about the telephone, as my letter will be quite enough to look after it. You see, if they do have the telephone taken out, it will cost me an awful lot of money to have it put in again.
>
> Yours sincerely,
> Helen Fowles.

Activity 17

Study the examples given in 2.7 below and discuss some of them in small groups. **Rewrite** one or more of them in accordance with your teacher's instructions.

Activity 18

Set out this letter from the electrical contractor on the basis that the only total figure quoted allows for all the omissions and additions required by the plumber and the customer.

The stiff tone of business letters may often reflect anxiety felt by the writer for whom writing is not a common activity. It is a paradox, but the feeling that writing letters is difficult can itself make it more difficult. One reason for the difficulty is that the writer sets out to draft his text without having worked out how to organise it. Having the content and ideas straight in your mind usually requires that you have them straight in a set of preparatory notes. Here is an example of what happens when that is not done:

F. H. Bunce Ltd.
ELECTRICAL CONTRACTORS
27, Station Road
West Stanton
Sussex

Dear Madam,

   Enclosed please find estimate for Electrical work requested in two copies. Price quoted includes £14 for Dimplex heater in bathroom as well as £6 for bulkhead fitting in porch and £5 for globe-type fitting in bathroom.

   While making estimate you telephoned to say you would not want cooker point (£28.50) or immersion heater wiring (£17) but these are included in my quoted total of £405.60 for complete rewire. While in house the plumber mentioned time clock and local wiring for boiler control which I have not included in my estimate but would cost £20 for the one and £10-£15 for other.

   Kitchen figure includes cost of Fluo light fitment.

                    Yours faithfully,

                    F. H. Bunce

Many students of business studies have allowed their courses in law to frighten them about the proper tone and style of business documents. It is perfectly true that an estimate constitutes an offer of a price, and the letter accepting an estimate is an instruction to carry out work and undertaking to pay for it. The fact that letters may have legal force, however, does not itself require them to be formal and stiff. It does require them to be clear, and that is part of the objection to some of the examples given. We can see this even more clearly in the case of formal reports like a survey of a building, where the surveyor may be liable in law for inaccuracies or omissions. Again, that does not have to make his writing stiff:

>   I did not see any evidence of
> woodworm or dry rot, but it was not
> possible to lift the floor cover-
> ings in each room for a thorough
> inspection of this point.
>   The joists and flooring of the front
> ground floor room, as seen from the
> cellar, were in good condition.

It is quite unnecessary to express this in the stilted form 'Evidence was not perceived of woodworm or dry rot . . .'

You may work for an organisation which has particular rules or 'house styles'. We know of one employer who forbids the use of passive verbs, although his original instruction to the staff read 'the use of passive verbs in letters and memoranda is forbidden'. Another employer requires all letters to be composed by assembling sentences from a manual. There are, of course, few easy or simple rules about good letter writing, and regulations of this kind are unlikely to make the job easier.

2.6 Formal personal letters

There is a range of letters concerning personal business which are neither person–person nor firm–firm, but need to be fairly formal even though writer and reader may know each other quite well. Consider Helen Fowles' situation in answering a request from a fellow student to be allowed to rent a room in her house. The arrangement can be an informal and 'friendly' one, but that basis could put the tenant in the position of not knowing some fairly important information. For example, does the rent cover the gas bills as well as the rates? If this kind of question is left unresolved, relationships could suffer when the gas bills arrive.

Activity 19

Assume that Mary MacGuire is a student in the same year as Helen and that they know each other by name but not well. **Write the letter** in which Helen would set out for Mary the terms of any tenancy in her house, but saying that the precise rent is not to be fixed until July of the preceding term.

Activity 20

Helen Fowles has inherited her parents' house in Windsor and sold it, and placed the proceeds of the sale in the Ledsham Branch of the Broadstone Building Society, whose Branch Manager has become one of her most trusted guides and friends. She has to ask the Manager of the Ledsham Branch of the Building Society to arrange for £2,000 to be transferred from her Building Society account to her current account at the bank (National Westminster Bank, Ledsham Central Branch) to cover the cost of the building and wiring work. **Write the letter required.**

2.7 Examples

The examples which follow are typical of actual business correspondence, and are not intended as models to be followed. They are intended to provide

1. examples of layout and arrangement for discussion in the light of the guidance already given
2. examples of how to organise the content or message, which is the subject of our own commentary given after each letter. These comments do not deal with all the points worth discussing.

A

```
                              W. P. DARTON & Co.
                              169 Ledsham High Road
                              Arledon


                              May  14  1979
Dear Madam.

We thank you for your letter of 14th requesting
estimates for works at 16 Butter Lane Ledsham
and your subsequent telephone call.  We prepared
estimates as instructed and give amendments made
pursuant to telephone call separately as we under-
stand from your call you did not wish us to revisit
the property to complete estimate.  It will be seen
that full central heating would cost £687 more than
the alternative proposed, which is not recommended.

We have referred items 16-22 to our neighbours
Messrs W.H.Churcher & Co, Electrical Engineers,
who will submit estimate separately.

            Yours sincerely,

              W. L. Darton.
         (sgd)   W L Darton
```

The writer of this letter actually took the telephone call referred to himself, and gets into a remarkable tangle trying to avoid saying so. This arises from the notion, once a very widespread one, that business letters should never say 'I'. Logically they should not say 'you' either! He takes a liberty about the electrical work without apologising. Much more grave is the omission of the comma after £687, transforming the meaning of the sentence, and his next clause does not make clear what it is that is not recommended.

B

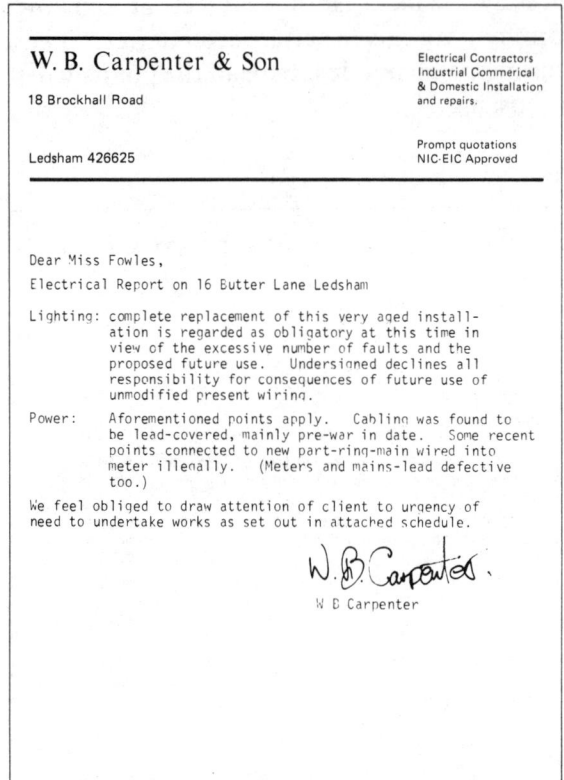

'Dear Miss Fowles' is correct; omission of 'Yours sincerely' is incorrect. The writer has met the recipient because she was in the house to let him in for inspection, so his style is too formal. It would carry much more urgency if he wrote:

'The wiring is old and dangerous and should be replaced as soon as you can arrange it. Some of the power points are wired to a recent ring-main, but even that is not properly wired to the meter. The rest of the wiring, for lighting and power, is full of leaks, some of them serious. The bulk of the wiring has not been touched for forty years.'

Considered as an Electrical Report (Carpenter's own heading) it is defective. The conclusion and recommendation are very clear, but nothing is said about the type of tests employed and not enough evidence is given to show that the survey was thorough.

The 'no-responsibility' clause is not necessary.

C

Business letters of this quaint formality are still occasionally written. The flowery grace of the second paragraph comes close to the continental practice, where the courtesies are much more elaborate. The stiltedness of the first paragraph stems from Haskins' belief that business English has to be impersonal, which is quite untrue.

It would help Mr. Haskins and others like him if he could and would write simple, direct forms such as:

'I have inspected the plumbing and heating system and attach my report and estimate. I have followed your numbered list, omitting electricals but adding two items which I think you will wish to consider. The work is straightforward and I would very much like the job.'

D

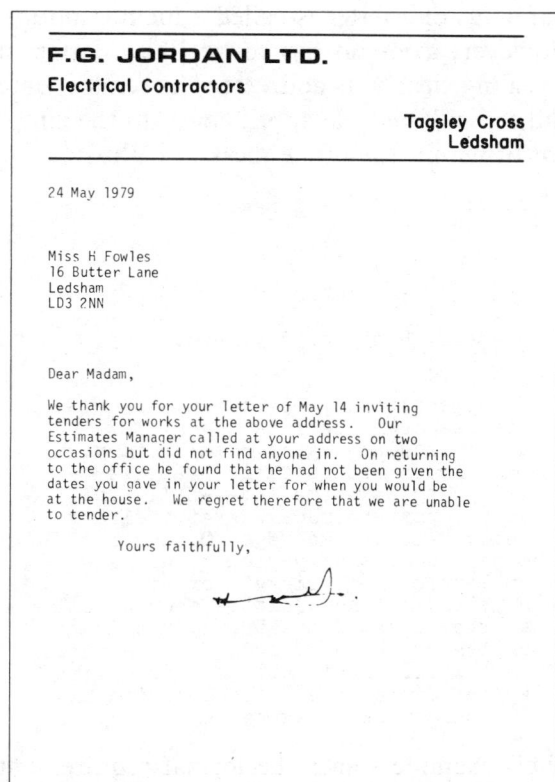

A model of the effective business letter, which treats the addressee as intelligent enough to have a mind of her own. He has made notes on his conversation and has remembered to give Helen the advice she sought on a heating system. The offer in the last paragraph is perfectly good business, but Henderson has to guard against the client thinking he is too 'sharp'. He has realised that most of his work comes from people who judge by the man rather than by his prices.

E

Activity 21

Discuss in small groups how Helen Fowles would view letter E above, and whether the firm sending it could have improved it.

2.8 Memoranda

Between separate firms or separate individuals in private life, written communication is naturally by letter. Within the same firm, however, it is wasteful to use the company letterhead and an envelope. A written note from colleague to colleague without the usual trappings of a letter is called a memorandum. However, a memo has to be like a letter in revealing clearly its addressee, its sender, date and topic. This rule applies even to the simplest of within-the-office messages, thus:

```
From:     General Manager

To:       All staff paid on hourly-rate

Date:     September 10, 1979

Subject:  Bank holidays etc.
```

```
It appears that the company has made a
mistake over the rate of pay for the
day following August Bank Holiday.  It
was agreed with workers' represent-
atives to pay time-and-a-half, but the
actual payment made was at ordinary
daily rates.  The Wages Office has
made its list of payments due, and
employees who believe they are
entitled to the addition should call
at the Wages Office during the lunch
or tea breaks on Tuesday and Wednesday
next week.  Don't all go at once, and
agreed payments will be included in
the same week's pay packet.
```

This example shows the format requirements of a memorandum plainly:

1. from
2. to
3. date
4. subject } always in this order
5. reference if any
6. content
7. signature (when required)

The *content* should include four elements:

6a. a tie-in or link: the opening sentence should refer to a previous communication or a known event

6b. what the writer wants his readers to know or do (or both)

6c. whatever the reader needs, as information or guidance, in order to understand 6b or carry out the writer's wishes

6d. a clear statement of when the reader should do as asked.

Many business firms use a prepared 'memo pad', which may also have sets of 'instruction terms' telling the reader what he has to do (eg 'For your information' or 'for signature') or what the reader should do with the memo itself. In many firms this 'memo pad' also doubles as an attachment slip, for pinning to other papers with an instruction about what should be done with them. Here is an example:

```
NOUNSHIRE COUNTY COUNCIL
SOCIAL SERVICES DEPARTMENT
(Northern Area)

From                          To

Date

  [ ] for action              [ ] please draft reply
  [ ] for information         [ ] please discuss
  [ ] for your comments       [ ] previous corresp. please
  [ ] for your approval       [ ] as you requested
  [ ] for your signature      [ ] PLEASE RETURN
                              [ ] file

Subject.

_____

Reply on this side or overleaf if necessary.
```

2.8.1 Using the context

Memoranda occur within firms and organisations. They therefore arise between writers and recipients who know a good deal of each other's business. The difference between a letter, where such knowledge cannot be taken for granted, and a memorandum, can be seen in an example:

```
From:     General Manager
To:       Manager Plumbing
Date:     July 4 1979
Subject:  16 Butter Lane, Ledsham
          (Contract 2669S)

You are scheduled for this job between
15.8 and 10.9 and we are committed to
meeting later limit as final stage of
a big s-w job.  Customer has notified
that previous occupant has left and
solicitors have agreed to her having
work started.  I know you have it
scheduled, but if you could advance
we would gain because trowel-trades
are starting 19.7 or 20.7 and a long
gap between parts of a job makes us
look a bit foolish.  Tell me what you
can do.
```

    The comparatively informal tone and the clipped language are only part of the differences from a letter: some of the wording arises from the situation – 'advance' here means 're-schedule' rather than 'speed up'; *s-w* (i.e. small-works) is an abbreviation within the trade.

    There are dangers, of course: these qualities in memoranda, which need to be as informal as clarity and explicitness will allow, can be a serious handicap when the writer assumes a shared-knowledge which his reader does not have. Here one of the plumbers fitting a boiler in the kitchen at 16 Butter Lane sends a Supplies Note back to the firm's yard:

From: W. Snaith, SW Plumbers
To: Stores
Date: 27.7.79
Contract & Job No: 2669S/18

This set of fittings won't work with the boiler supplied. Boiler goes neatly in the cupboard but the pipes supplied require me to drive straight through a 3ft 6ins chimney of solid brick. Please re-supply.

This memorandum assumes:

a. that the Stores knows which boiler he is writing about;
b. that Stores is in a position to know what to supply instead, even though Stores will never have seen a plan of the house;
c. that what has been supplied already does not form part of the complete set. The memo is a painful example of failure to be explicit.

3
Writing at work – notes and reports

3.1 Notes

Activity 18 revealed the value of preliminary planning when writing a business letter. The form which such plans take is usually called 'notes', but this term covers many varieties of actual text and many different purposes. The commonest is that of 'taking notes', i.e. writing down some parts of material which is given in spoken form such as a lecture. The ability to take one's own notes from a speaker is a skill which it is important to acquire. It is a totally different ability from that of writing down 'dictated notes' which are in common use in many schools. The following points concern 'own-use notes', the rough jottings which you (and virtually everyone else) will use to take down material which will subsequently be 'written up'.

3.1.1 Arrangement of notes

There are two essential features to 'own-use notes': layout and numbering. In the layout, sequences which belong together are put down together; groups of items which are separate from other groups of items are marked off from them visually on the page. It is quite normal for the layout of own-use notes to use abbreviations and omissions of all kinds, many of which may be comprehensible only to the person who wrote the notes (and sometimes not even then).

3.1.2 Numbering

The system of numbering to be used in hand-written own-use notes is partly up to the writer, but there are some useful guidelines. It is always worth watching, in the early part of a talk, for any signal that the speaker gives about the structure of the talk: if he says he is going to deal with four matters, that points to notes in four sections, each headed A to D. If section B has three parts, they too will be numbered, in a way which avoids confusion with the letter numbering A to D: the usual choice is (i) to (iii). If the sub-section B (ii) has two important points to keep separate, these again can be given a separate numbering to avoid confusion with the numbering 'higher up', thus: B(ii)a, and B(ii)b. It then becomes possible later on to refer to one of these points as B(ii)a rather than writing out the nature of the point in full. The principle involved in the numbering of notes is that each 'level' is given a distinctive kind of number pattern.

3.1.3 An example

Opposite are notes which Helen Fowles made on the house she eventually bought, at the time of her first visit before she had arranged for a survey or made an offer for it.

16 Butter Lane, L'm.
3 bed, brick, 1900+, no fr gdn, sm rear yard,
1 flwrbed
a. porch & frt dr OK
b. steep stairs, dark hall; lge front room OK (sashes)
   kitchen behind (both to R - house is a semi)
   11 x 11, stone sink & ckr in v cramped corner,
   tap nby.
       (Kitchen: what behind fireplace panel?
        uneven floor,? damp? Q-tiles, what on?
        back door u/s
        blt-in cpbds too shallow to be useful
c. back rm, sitting rm, bay window. OK.
d. upstairs - carpet on strs loose.
   sep WC (very classy for this date of house) flush
                                                  quiet
   bed 1 - big enough for 2!
   bed 2 - over kitchen, OK
   bed 3 - over back rm, suit a dwarf
   queries: state of sashes, damp from chimneys
e. bathrm - marv o-fash claw-ft bath, cold tank
   above it, hot taps a trickle - where heated? cold
   slow too. Basin sound if stained. Wastes fast & noisy
f. floors look good; paintwork vg ins, OK outs.
g. roof messy bt sound, chimney needs work (no pots)
   gutters look OK, front bay RWP broken, house walls
   sound, yard walls flaking badly.
h. Oddities: a basement! 12x9, dry, sound, brick floor,
   painted brick walls, joists ceiling (frnt rm floor
   looks good), steep steps, air vents, windows not poss
   Wld make a lovely TV room. Outside shed in back yard
   for bikes. Price is ridiculous, but the old lady hates
   it all and has taken a shine to me.
Summary: best yet; space, location, condition all ideal.
         much work to do, kitchen awkward, get survey.

3.1.4 Another example

Here are the notes made for Helen by a friend who visited another house for her:

> Gloomy out and in, peeling paper, unocc over yr. front & back dnstrs rms thrown into one (we'd have to rebuild the wall). The kitchen is tiny, damp, totally imposs for you to improve or us to use. But the price is stunning, though with improvement costs might be un-worthwhile.

You will notice the lack of detail – there is nothing about the bedrooms, for example; the absence of clear guidance to Helen about whether she should spend time looking at it; and the vagueness about the price and the house's value.

3.1.5 A professional's notes

When Helen called in a surveyor to inspect in detail and tell her what needed doing to the house described in her own notes (3.1.3 above), his notes on the cellar were like this:

> cellar, under front room, 12.9 x 8.8 x 6.4 brick flr, walls unplast, pntd brick, sound & dry ceiling open to grd-flr joists (free from wdwm/d.rot/damp) 2 eye-level clear air-vents to front, 10" above ground level mains elec metre by cellar door, no light or switch or power pt. short flt wooden steps from hallway, steps sound. Room remarkably dry and airy, no sign of damp in the past.

Activity 22

Here is an extract from the final report by the same surveyor. Study it with care and then **rewrite his notes** as the section of his report dealing with the cellar.

```
kitchen: 11'4" x 12'2"; two 13 amp power
points, central ceiling pendant switched from
hall doorway; quarry-tile floor set on earth
or sand; 5' x 3' sash window over sink, with
back door next to it.  Large chimney-breast
projects into room midway on S side, enclosed
with plywood panel which conceals a large,
unserviceable kitchen range of 1920's date
which once heated hot water by means of a
back boiler.  (Water now heated by immersion
heater, controlled from kitchen.)  The floor
shows many signs of rising damp, past
and present, and probably needs to be taken up
and re-set on a damp-proof cement or asphalt
screed.  The rear door is a lightweight glass-
panelled door fitted with hardboard panels on
both sides which have caused the door to warp
and slip on its hinges.  There is no other
sign of damp, worm, or rot in this room, and
the decorations, while dull, are very
adequate.
```

3.2 Reports

'Report' is a much misused word. When a Manager says to one of his staff, 'Give me a report on that', in nine cases out of ten what he intends is a memorandum, and as a rule that is what he receives. But managers suffer from the illusion that writing a report is a special skill which can easily be learned. Do not be deceived: it may take many years to become a good writer of reports. In this book we deal only with the most elementary kind.

3.2.1 Reports and memoranda

The central difference between a report and a memorandum is that the memorandum is intended for and written for the person it is addressed to, whereas a report is intended to be and likely to be read and used by many other people. The object of a report is to present information and views so that the people to whom it is directed may take appropriate action. In business, a report is usually asked for: if you have to write one it is in reply to an instruction or because the circumstances make it necessary.

3.2.2 The content of reports

Any report must satisfy two fundamental requirements:
1. The person who asks for it must be free to use it as he wishes: he must be free to cite it, quote from it, or send it to colleagues.
2. The text must distinguish clearly that which is fact, that which is personal opinion or judgement, that which is advice and recommendation, and that which is guesswork.

The first of these requirements may present problems. For example, you might not know who, other than the recipient, will see the report and this makes it difficult to judge what assumptions to make about your readers. In most practical circumstances you can assume the readership shares the technical knowledge and interests of your work-place. If you are preparing a report for elected members of a local council or committee, however, you may have to be more careful. These ladies and gentlemen may be laymen in technical matters but are sensitive about being patronised, so you have to assume that they know something about the topic of your report and will ask about technical terms if they need to.

3.3 Types of report

There are three main types of report:
Informing Reports. These, as their title suggests, are written to inform someone about something. Your supervisor may wish you to keep him informed about events which occur while you are carrying out a certain piece of business or the progress you have achieved on a task. You and your supervisor share a similar degree of knowledge of the work, and your report is thus a routine matter which may take place regularly. It will have the bare essentials of what your reader needs to know, and will not need to offer advice or recommendations. In format it may well look very like a memorandum.

Briefing Reports. These are necessary when a superior needs fuller information on a particular topic. The information is likely to be shared among a number of people making decisions as a result of what they read. It is not likely that you will have to prepare such documents while in a junior position, but you may have to help in assembling the material for them. The report is being produced in response to a request, so the nature of the request must be recorded at the beginning. The main body of the report presents the requested information with the utmost clarity, and the distinction between main points and less important ones needs to be enforced by paragraph numbering and indentation. Any briefing report provides information but need not offer advice, make recommendations or draw conclusions. If the report is lengthy (i.e. more than two pages of typescript) it is usual to supply a synopsis or summary at the beginning.

Advisory Reports. Advisory reports are almost always prepared by experts, who are commissioned to collect, sift and organise the data relevant to the exercise of a judgement or informed professional opinion. It is assumed from the start that the writer knows or will find out much more than his reader will ever wish to know. Such a report will begin by stating its terms of reference, i.e. why it is being written. It will give some indication of what the writer has done in order to write the report, unless he is relying entirely on his previous expert knowledge of the topic. The main body of such a report is referred to as the 'findings', and will lead logically to the conclusions, which should be brief. Thereafter the writer has to earn his keep by giving advice in the form of his 'recommendations'. This five-part structure (Terms of Reference, Procedure, Findings, Conclusions, Recommendations) is sometimes treated as the only correct or proper format for reports, but there is no truth in this claim. This format was originally developed in the Indian Civil Service in the early nineteenth century, and has been passed on through the Field Manuals of the Armed Services. It is a useful guide, but it is suitable only for advisory reports of considerable scale. Your own report writing, such as it is likely to be for some time, will need a much simpler framework such as:

Introduction
The facts
Conclusions

3.4 Report format

It cannot be too strongly emphasised that the format of a report needs to be dictated by its content. The traditional format given above is a useful guide in ordering that content into appropriate sections, but should not be treated as the only way in which a report can or should be set out. If the text of a report could give its essential substance in a 100-word memorandum, it is silly to try to spread this material into the full five-part format of a conventional report. Any report of whatever kind must set out to communicate clearly and economically and without ambiguity. The format in which it is expressed has to serve those objects and no others.

3.4.1 Content and format

The format of a report is, then, subsidiary to its content. The problem of assembling the information on which to base the report may be considerably more difficult than that of deciding its type or layout. You will need to learn how to investigate as an essential part of your course, and the activity given below lists a number of tasks which are very like the report-writing tasks arising in many business settings.

Activity 23

Deal with one or more of the questions opposite by assembling the necessary information and presenting it in an appropriately simple report. In each case, it is assumed that Helen Fowles has selected her four tenants, that they have all agreed to take part in getting the house ready for occupation, and that she is sending them some of these questions and instructions.

3.5 Reporting style

One element in reporting has little to do with format or content: reports often cite other sources or quote observations by other people. For example, let us suppose that near the end of the building work on 16 Butter Lane the foreman left Helen a note thus:

We have a problem. The carpet-layer came to do the bedrooms and when my men came back from lunch they found a note from him saying I have put a nail through a waterpipe in the bedroom at the back and there's a small leak. I haven't pulled out the nail in case it makes a flood but I have turned off the water. I can't get the plumber back until Friday and I have left the water back off until then. I hope this isn't going to be inconvenient for you.

If you read this carefully you may be able to tell where the quotation from the carpet layer's note begins, but you will have some difficulty telling where it ends. Are the last two sentences written by the foreman to Helen or by the carpet layer to the foreman? The original note in fact consisted of only two sentences, ending at 'turned off the water'. We have to find ways of making this sort of distinction clear. There are two possibilities – quotation and reported form. We shall assume in this book that quotation, i.e. the punctuation of

---

1. I had intended to use my parents' old electric cooker, but it is too big to go into the space in the chimney breast in the kitchen. To judge from the newspaper small ads, we could get a decent gas cooker for £40 and a decent electric cooker for £25. On the assumption that we are going to live in the house for three years, which is the better bet?

2. Jenny: we have four bedrooms, kitchen and sitting room – and no curtains. I heard curtain-making was up your street, and I'd gladly pay you a proper rate if you are interested. I'm buying the material, I have a thing about liking them lined, and at a pinch would have them made by the shop where I get the material. Can you find out what the shops charge for making up and see if a figure of say two thirds of that would be a fair one to pay you for the job.

3. Mary: we are all going to need bookshelves, and I think they will have to go on the walls because floorspace is short. Would you look into the systems and brands and see if anything better than a stack of orange boxes is even remotely affordable. We each need about 1.5 metres, and I expect it's the boards themselves which run up the cost.

4. Jean: the builder is murmuring about insulating the loft. This is about 400 sq ft and the insulation has to go between the joists – the builder says they are the usual distance apart. What would insulation save if we all use gas fires? What would insulation cost? I did hear there was a grant scheme.

5. An uncle sent me £10 telling me to buy a few books about home making and household repairs on a budget. What am I to spend it on that you would find useful?

6. The sitting room has two easy chairs, and there are going to be five of us. I can't abide torn and scuffed upholstery. Would you work out what we ought to get to sit on and what it would cost.

7. The estate agent told me the house has a rateable value of £120.50. He said this wasn't what we would pay in rates – that would be less, but there is a separate water and sewage rate. What is 'rateable value' and what is the rate we pay?

direct speech, is something which you learned at school and can brush up with your teacher by studying the examples given elsewhere in this book. Reported form, which avoids quotation marks, has to do other things instead:

The carpet layer wrote, 'I have put a nail through a pipe'.
The carpet layer wrote that he had put a nail through a pipe.

He went on, 'I haven't pulled out the nail because there might be a flood, but I have turned off the water.'
He added that he had not pulled out the nail in order to prevent a flood, but had turned off the water.

3.6 Reported form

Not all reported material originates in speech, and we are therefore referring to it as 'reported form' rather than 'reported speech'. Its rules are straight-forward:

1. 'I' forms (I, we, me etc.) become 'he/she' forms (grammatically, first and second person move to third person)
2. 'Is' and 'are' forms become 'was' and 'were' forms (present tense becomes past tense)
3. 'Will' forms and 'am going to' forms become 'would' forms (future becomes conditional)
4. 'Have' forms become 'had' forms
5. Colloquial forms become formal

Thus, 'I have put a nail through a pipe' becomes:
He reported that he had punctured a pipe with a nail.

'You'll have to switch your plans, I'm afraid' becomes:
He said he regretted that she would have to change her plans.

'Did you switch your plans?' asked Joe becomes:
Joe asked her whether she had changed her plans.

In practice very few conversations in business life are ever recorded or reported complete. If the precise words employed are themselves in dispute, the conversations will normally be given verbatim (word-for-word). Almost invariably, the reporting of events or discussions entails condensing as well as reporting. Sometimes this compression is very considerable, so that a six-hour bargaining session over a wage dispute might be reported quite simply as 'The meeting failed to reach agreement'. The following transcriptions are drawn from real life situations, and in each case the meeting has to be reported – i.e. it has *both* to be put into reported form *and* appropriately abbreviated. The length of the resulting summary may be discussed, but cannot be laid down in advance.

Transcript A

Helen Fowles telephones the solicitor in Ledsham who is dealing with the purchase of the house. It is not yet complete, but the vendor has agreed to let her have the keys to start the building work. She wrote to the agent authorising him to release the keys to the builder, but the agent refused to do so. She has to get her solicitor to move quickly by contacting the vendor's solicitor for authority to release the keys. The message she leaves on the answer-phone is as follows, and your task is to **type it up for the solicitor.**

Helen: I'm sorry to trouble you, but we have a blockage. Robinson, my builder, went to get the 16 Butter Lane keys from Dawson's today. I had written them to say they could hand the keys to him instead of me. They refused. We have no authority to release the keys, they said. This is really rather annoying, and I wondered how quickly you could get something done to have Dawson's get the message from the vendor's solicitor.

Transcript B

The local inspector for a major insurance firm usually has a trainee with him when he sees clients, and in this case Helen has gone in to arrange the details of cover on the house. The trainee records the important parts of the conversation, and the Inspector asks her to convert the notes into a letter confirming Helen's instruction. **Write that letter.**

Insp: You have read our prospectuses carefully, I gather.
Helen: Yes, and I want to arrange three distinct parts of the insurance – the house itself, my furniture and fittings, and my personal things.
Insp: What about the tenants?
Helen: They arrange their own. I'll tell them you offer a good discount.
Insp: Do you have a proper valuation for the house?
Helen: Yes: the surveyor said on the phone yesterday that I ought to insure the house for £12,000. Yes, I know you've got it down as £7,700 but it ought to go up at once.
Insp: Very well. The policy to be index-linked?
Helen: No: I will probably be in the house for only three years, and will adjust the value each time I renew.
Insp. Very well. What figure do you want for the contents?
Helen: £700.
Insp: Are you sure that's enough? It sounds a very small sum.
Helen: There are five new beds worth £40 each, about £100-worth of old furniture bought from the old owner, as much furniture again bought from second-hand shops, and the cooker and fridge which are worth about £40 each. It doesn't add up to much.
Insp: Curtains? Light fittings? Shades? Pictures? Cushions – don't you think you should go round every room when it's all set up, make a list and put a figure on each item?
Helen: Well, yes, all right. Can we fix it at £850 to be going on with?
Insp: Very good. And your personal possessions?
Helen: Jewellery worth £900, valued for probate six months ago when my mother died. A gold watch, a fair stack of books; and my clothes.
Insp: The point here is you need cover for these things at replacement cost not present value, and you need cover for them out of the house as well as in, right? That means what we call an All Risks policy, and any single item worth £100 or more has to be listed separately. You'll do that for me? Thank you. And you'll let me have the list and scope of the cover with this form? I'm putting the property policy application form in here as well, but the house is insured even though the form hasn't come in yet.

Transcript C

Here the students who want to move into Helen's house with her are discussing the problem with her. Your task is to **report the outcome** to the family solicitor in Windsor who is keeping a fatherly eye on Helen's housing. The four students are Jane, Sarah, Maggie and Nonna.

Helen: Well, I hadn't really intended taking on as many as four. It's quite a small house you know. How come you aren't fixed up yet?

Sarah: We were going to be taking on a big flat from Nonna's brother, but he's decided to take the union job and stay on.
Nonna: Oh, Sarah! It's not a *big* flat: Helen's house is three times the size.
Helen: But there are only three rooms upstairs and three down, one of them the kitchen.
Jane: Yes, but how big are the rooms? The small bedrooms are about 10×11 aren't they? But the big one is 14×11, and so's the front room underneath it.
Maggie: What Jane's driving at, Helen, is that you have one of the big rooms and she and I share the other. It's big enough.
Helen: Oh, I hadn't thought of that.
Nonna: That way you keep the back room by the kitchen as a common sitting room.
Helen: Which I was going to do anyway. But suppose you two sharers don't get on?
Sarah: They've got on for the last year in a room no bigger, and if it doesn't work we can take turns to share.
Helen: And the rent?
Sarah: Same figure for all four of us, whether sharing or not. We'll all have the same shares of bath and loo and common room and heat.
Helen: That all right by the others?
All: Yes.
Helen: But nothing about the sharing bit in the written agreement?
Sarah: Not really necessary, I'd say.

Transcript D

Builder's office secretary recording the plumber's observations on 16 Butter Lane before preparation of estimate. Her tape is here transcribed in full: **prepare a list of items for pricing.**

Want the details, Mary? OK. 16 Butter Lane, yes? Well, it's antique: lead piping mostly with bits of copper here and there. Cistern in the bathroom and obviously a lot of scale in the cold pipes - only a trickle from each tap. Hot supply is immersion, in a tiny copper cyl on a shelf in the middle bedroom. Feeds bathroom - no hot pipe to kitchen at all. Owner says there used to be a back boiler in kitchen but not used now - the range is still there, about 40 years old. Have to quote for new cistern and complete repipe job. About 180 ft run but it's quite simple to fit, unless cistern goes in roof which would mean a new loft hole. Existing cistern's in bathroom, too small and probably unsafe. The lady won't want that sink - it's stone, and cracked. Go for new top, new unit, proper taps. Bathroom fittings and san ware quite usable. Separate WC in good nick. You'll have to include taking out the range and making good - could be quite a job that.

4
Writing at work

This chapter deals chiefly with writings which are intended to be read by people who may be unknown to the writer. These include notices, announcements, instructions, circulars, form letters and the like. As with previous chapters, we shall base most of our examples and activities on a particular situation, which is described at the beginning of the main body of the chapter.

4.1 Notices, announcements and circulars

The English language is used very widely for communicating with large numbers of people who do not know the writer who is addressing them. This may seem a very ordinary fact, but historically speaking it is a very new one, and many people are still quite unused to it. We see this every time we observe that somebody who is quite happy to receive a hand-written letter is puzzled or disturbed at receiving a printed or duplicated one. The readiness with which people attribute all kinds of documents to 'them' is further evidence of the fact that the era of mass communication is still only very incomplete: very large numbers of people do not like to be communicated with as if they were part of the mass.

4.1.1

A particular example of the problems involved in group communication occurs in notices and announcements. We treat notices as different from announcements: in this book, an announcement seeks to convey information, while a notice sets out to direct or guide behaviour. For example:

Announcements
DEEP END
Bridge 14′ 6″
Ungated Crossing

Notices
Keep off the grass
Please pass down the car
Keep out of reach of childen

The distinction between conveying information and controlling behaviour, however, is often blurred – at times deliberately:

Ladies Only
Trespassers will be Prosecuted
Emergency Handle Penalty £5
Shoplifting is not worth it

It is sometimes hard to tell whether the reader is being told about something or told to do or not to do something. In the last sixty years there has been a very sharp change in the readiness of people who write notices for public places to be definite and commanding in their tone. Many notices now have some kind of attempt at being a little more human. A weekly magazine once ran a competition which made fun of this tendency by inviting 'nice' or 'courteous' versions of these rather rude and curt commandments. The winning entry came from L. E. Jones:

> This compartment is set aside for Ladies who wish to travel without Gentlemen. British Railways feel confident that Gentlemen who wish to travel with Ladies will readily understand that Ladies who wish to travel without Gentlemen are not the kind of Ladies with whom Gentlemen who wish to travel with Ladies would wish to travel.

Again, a couple living in a country village with an expanse of unfenced grass in front of their house found the neighbours' dogs a great nuisance. They tried 'Keep off the Grass' without effect. The local highways department refused to allow them to put up a fence. 'Keep your dogs on a lead' did not work either. Then, one day, the couple had a triumph. They put up a tiny, typed notice which read,

```
        THIS IS TO ANNOUNCE THAT
          WE HAVE BEEN AWARDED
             FIRST PRIZE
         IN THE COMPETITION FOR
   THE COUNTRY'S BEST-KEPT DOGS' LOO
```

4.2 The setting

For the purposes of this chapter you are George Macy, aged 18, and employed as a wages clerk in the personnel department of Ramsey and Foxdale Ltd., manufacturers of parts and sub-assemblies for electrical components in the vehicle trades. The firm employs 495 people, 82 of them women, all of them on a single day shift. You are a keen all-round athlete, and were very flattered to be asked to undertake the post of assistant secretary to the company's sports club. In due course you find out that the club has a committee of eight members, with a chairman, vice-chairman and a secretary. The secretary is an efficient, bossy little man in his late forties, who believes quite rightly that he is not very good with a pen, and who supposes that he can safely leave most of the clerical and writing side of the secretaryship to you. The club does not, in fact, have a treasurer, since the members have a subscription deducted from their wage packet by the firm, and the company accountant undertakes to meet all the expenditures of the club and is a member of the club's committee. The company is a self-governing unit with its own board of directors, but is owned by an American manufacturer of much larger scale It sends a number of its trainees from other subsidiaries in various parts of the world to spend periods of one and two years with Ramsey and Foxdale both to learn the business and to improve its production performance.

4.2.1

On taking up your duties, you agree with the secretary to spend two hours after work each Tuesday working on the club's records and trying to put its paperwork in order. You discover that in spite of the company's payroll, there are fewer than 100 members of the sports club whose subscriptions have been paid. The names are given below in the order in which they appear in the card index drawer. Study this list, and go through it with detailed attention to the separate tasks listed.

Activity 24

1. Scan the list for at least ten names (other than those at the end of the list) which are misplaced in their alphabetical order according to the second letter of the name.
2. Do likewise for at least ten names which are misplaced in their alphabetical order

Ambari	Khan	Richard
Asbridge	King	Reivel
Ashford	Keene	Scorr
Astle	Knight	Scorer
Aslam	Kneale	Schoor
Birkett	Langley	Schutz
Bartles	Langham	Schlegel
Brough	Lee	Shotter
Bristol	Le Mesurier	Singh L. M.
Compton	La Salle	Singh, V. R.
Campian	MacLean	Singh, V. S.
Cook	McQuaid	Smith W. R.
Corderey	Macquarie	Smith J. M.
Coote	Mackinlay	Smith-Hales
Cousins	McAllister	Smith B. V.
Delargy	Maw	Smith J. K. R.
De La Hay	Moore	Szabo
De Montford	Mukherjee	Takamoto
Empingham	Murray	Tagimitzu
Emmott	Moray	Tailor
Firman	Narayan	Ulyatt
Fillmore	Norman	Udall
Friend	Normand	Vallins
Freestone	Patel	Quinn
Galt	Potter	Vallient
Gall	Overton	Lall
Grey	Pound	Verity
Grayling	Porterhouse	Verey
Gleeve	Pestell	Jones D. L.
Harris	Powers	Imrie
Harrington	Povey	Adley
Hooker	Pozzi	Target
Hoare	Pozzoli	Heussmann
Jones, B. M.	Ricards	Johns
Johnson		Jones C. W.

according to the third letter of the name.

3. Scan the list for those names misplaced in their alphabetical order by the fourth or a subsequent letter of the name.

4. Insert in their proper alphabetical position in the list those names at the end of the list which are clearly misplaced.

(*Note: the standard guidance on alphabetic ordering of proper names can be found at the beginning of any Post Office telephone directory.*)

If you have found this exercise a very difficult one, do not be surprised: only a minority of adults ever find alphabetical order easy to handle without having learned systematically how to scan this kind of list. It is particularly important that any students who find this activity difficult attempt the tasks in the order given without skipping the first or second elements. The principles which apply to the alphabetical ordering of names also apply to the alphabetic ordering of words in general.

4.3 Notes and instructions

The second item immediately on George Macy's agenda has to do with a number of notices and announcements which the club secretary was on the point of issuing and which he has decided to ask George to improve upon. The text of each of these is given below.

A

The Committee has decided to do team selection every Tuesday night and to post the teams then. The team captains will arrange it so as selections for different teams don't clash.

B

In previous years fixture lists have been printed, but were having trouble getting fixtures booked ahead enough to get a list out early in the season.

C

Colleagues will be very sad to hear that Wilfred Harrington of the Circuits Inspection Team collapsed and died early yesterday evening. The funeral is to be completely private. Members who wish to contribute in his memory should please do so through the office charity box, and contributions received in the next seven days will be treated as gifts in memory of Wilfred. I will consult Mrs. Harrington about her choice of what charity to send it to.

D

Memo to the Bar Serving Team. Personnel have sent us a confidential note about Mary Aylings (Wages). She suffers from Petit Mal, which they call a mild form of Epilepsy. She takes the proper drug for it every day, and takes part in all ordinary office work. She may have occasional absences from work, but the important point for us is that she must not be allowed to take any alcoholic liquor. We are asked not to talk about it.

E

Notice to section heads, club organisers, members of social committee. We are getting into an impossible situation about the lounge and committee rooms in the social centre. The warden tells me that a lot of clashes are occurring because one or more of the groups intending to use the rooms has not confirmed the booking with him. There is more to this than your own convenience about meetings: the warden likes to arrange for supplies of tea and coffee and he has the cleaning to organise afterwards, so please co-operate.

F

Buxtite Ltd. have had to cancel Saturday's game with our Second XI and postpone the first team until July 14th owing to the industrial action at their works.

Activity 25

After discussion in class, **write improved versions** of two or more of these texts.

4.3.1 Written announcements

A number of these examples give illustrations of the problems involved in trying to use written announcements to control or guide how people behave. For written announcements which are designed to convey information to a large number of people, there are three basic guidelines:

1. if the person writing knows and is known to a majority of the people for whom the announcement is being written, the announcement should always be signed by the writer. Nothing is more damaging to human communications between people who know

one another than the use of unsigned forms of communication.

2. the text of an announcement should always assume, in the way it is written, that the reader and the writer are known to one another. In particular, as long as the announcement is giving information and not instructions, it should address the reader as 'you'.

3. if the information given in the announcement is likely to be unwelcome, the announcement should contain an explanation or an apology or both.

4.3.2 Notices

We do not give any further space to notices here, because it is exceedingly difficult to control or direct the behaviour of people by written notices. Even the most mature and experienced writers often fail to achieve the necessary level of tact.

Activity 26

Collect a large number of examples of notices (as distinct from announcements) and subject them to detailed analysis in class in order to see why they so regularly fail and why so often they give offence.

4.3.3 Instructions

Again, written instructions for the carrying-out of even quite simple manual tasks are very much more difficult to write successfully than they seem. Consider, for example, the standard sheet of instructions issued through retailers about how to wire a 13-amp plug, or the rather more complex assembly instructions for a piece of home-assembly furniture. A more elaborate example still is the instructions given in a dressmaking pattern. All of these examples and a great many others use diagrammatic illustration. Writing even quite simple instructions without any diagrams at all is almost impossible, unless the task is very simple indeed. Where diagrams cannot be used, it is wise to rely on the principle that nothing whatever can be taken for granted, the reader cannot be assumed to have any prior knowledge, and that it will be necessary to guide the reader's every movement at every stage.

Activity 27

For this Activity either write down absolutely clear written instructions for the task in hand or sit back to back with a colleague and **give the necessary instructions orally**. Examples of tasks suitable for this include:

changing a fountain pen cartridge
explaining how to sew a flat-felled seam
fixing any type of snap-fastener
fitting a new washer to a bicycle pump
assembling a fishing rod
making a set of eyelets
taking a car through a coin-operated car-wash

4.3.4 Oral instructions

We have already mentioned the problems of giving directions in the street. The following activities deal with other aspects of giving oral instructions.

Activity 28

Work to be arranged for individuals or pairs:

a. Put yourself in the position of a news reader on BBC Radio who has to announce that a poisonous gas has contaminated the national pipe network carrying natural gas from the North Sea. He then has to instruct every listener to turn off the gas supply to his own house at the mains and to explain to some viewers precisely what 'the mains' might mean.

b. As a radio announcer, explain in a period of extreme shortage of water how to save the water consumption of lavatory systems by fitting either a brick or a plastic bag itself full of water inside the cistern.

c. As a local radio announcer, you have to give news of a broken gas main in the centre of the nearest town. You have to inform listeners of a usable route through the town which avoids the area of the break. Base the answer on the map of a town known to you.

4.3.5 Receiving instructions

The examples in the previous activity make use of radio as the setting, but most oral instructions are given face-to-face. The person who is being instructed may either be inert and helpless or can co-operate in the process. In particular, when he is unsure of some point he can ask questions. The quality of the questions you ask when given instructions is often the clearest evidence of your own ability at oral communication. So if your teacher sets out to sharpen this ability by having the class engage in games such as Twenty Questions, do not dismiss this as mere fun: a skilful player of such questioning games is demonstrating one of the supreme skills of language – that of drawing conclusions from the most slender but logical evidence.

4.4 Meetings

A special form of group communication is the work of servicing a group which meets regularly such as a committee. There are special procedural rules governing the papers which bring together and record the work of a meeting (its agenda and minutes), which are dealt with more fully in our *People in Touch*. The essential skills at this level are to have a basic understanding of committee and meeting procedure, and the ability to make effective notes for writing up as the minutes.

4.4.1

Meetings must be conducted in an orderly fashion, following an order of business set out in advance, under the chairman's control. There is thus a convention that all who speak at a meeting address the chairman. Because some members may fail to do this, meetings sometimes become entangled in problems of procedure, which are usually referred to in the subsequent minutes in the briefest possible way.

4.4.2 Minutes

A meeting's minutes should record its decisions, not its discussions, unless the meeting decides otherwise. The minutes may thus be very brief, and are always cast in 'reported form' (on which see Section 2.6). Some meetings will occasionally decide that particular items be 'not minuted', while others may require particular items to be minuted in detail.

4.4.3 Taking the minutes

Young employees are liable to be told to 'take the minutes' of a meeting without knowing either the members or the business. It is always reasonable to ask to be excused this duty at your first meeting of a group which has met before. But if you are given the job,

1. sit next to someone who knows all the members by name.
2. do not even try to record everything word for word.

3. do record word-for-word the motions, amendments and resolutions proposed: you may well be asked to read them back.
4. develop a quick shorthand for most common decisions (such as agrd; carrd; item x qstnd by . . .).

Taking the minutes of a meeting is a sustained task of making a written summary from continuous spoken discourse. It is thus a very much harder task than it may seem. The following may help in acquiring the skills involved:

Activity 29

a. Listen to a *radio* news bulletin, preferably Radio 4, lasting for 13 minutes, making brief notes as you do so. After the bulletin, expand your notes as you think necessary and **write a summary** of the news bulletin in not more than 300 words.
b. **Repeat this exercise** with a different bulletin (but of the same overall length), and make a summary of not more than 150 words.
c. After you have done the previous exercises with radio, **attempt either or both of them with television.**
d. Listen, using sound only, to radio or TV news broadcasts of the same approximate scale on two different channels, preferably a BBC one and an ITV one. Without attempting to summarise the news itself, **write up in 150–200 words** the main differences in emphasis or treatment between the two bulletins.
e. Listen to a discussion, argument, or dispute between two or (at most) three colleagues at work or in a class, and after it has finished try to make a single minute of record **summarising the outcome.** Further valuable practice is offered in the final part of Chapter 2.

4.4.4 *Revision and editing*

Even very experienced writers of minutes will find it valuable to go through their version with someone else who was present before having the minutes written up and circulated to the members. This process of revision and editing of one's writing is referred to many times in this book, and nowhere is it more valuable than in learning how to take minutes. Remember that there is no fixed set of rules about what minutes ought to be like: each committee can make its own rules.

4.5 Circulars, forms and questionnaires

If we have something which we wish to convey in writing to more than a small number of people, instead of writing to each of them individually we can write one letter, reproduce copies of it, and send those. Such duplicated letters or memoranda are usually known as circulars.

The first question to ask about a circular is whether it is necessary. The second question is whether a circular is suited to the task in hand. It is easily forgotten that unless a circular is printed, it will come to the reader as a duplicated sheet without a personal salutation or signature. There are some people who believe that nobody should send a circular to anyone who has not previously received a personally signed letter from him. We sympathise, but the advice is hardly practical. Even so, the advice points up the acute problem of tone in circulars: people do not like being treated like sheep, and object to being ordered about, especially in writing.

4.5.1

The purposes which a circular can fulfil efficiently are very limited:

1. it can convey a *very limited* amount of factual information
2. it can convey a writer's attitude to conduct on the part of people whom the writer already knows personally.

What circulars *cannot* do effectively are:
3. convey complex information with any certainty that many readers will absorb it
4. convey rebuke, directives, or prohibitions
5. convey information or messages which mean widely differing things for different readers.

4.5.2

Circulars are like announcements in needing to meet one important but neglected criterion: they need to be readable by people who have a reading age of less than 10. (Mass-circulation newspapers meet this standard as a matter of course.)

Activity 30

1. **Select** part or all of the current prospectus of your own college of further education, and analyse it closely to see whether a reader of low reading attainment would be able to follow it.
2. As an extreme case, **inspect the safety provisions** in your own college or school building to see how far an adult illiterate would be able to act on them.
3. Select some examples of circular text which seem to you particularly hard on the weak reader, and **re-write** them so that an average child of 11 could understand them. Examples might include a Tax Return, the current forms of application for a passport or a driving licence, and the published regulations governing the entitlement of students to unemployment benefit.

4.5.3 Application forms

Circulars are designed to send information from a centre to a large number of people outside it. Forms, especially application forms, serve the reverse purpose of bringing the information to the centre. We set out on the opposite page two examples of an application form. The form itself is typical of those used by many employers for young applicants. In one case it is filled in thoroughly badly; and in the other is filled in adequately rather than well.

Activity 31

Copy out a full-size blank of this application form and after discussion of the two examples given, **complete your blank.**

Activity 32

Working in pairs, *either*:

a. **design a form** of application for membership of the Ramsey & Foxdale Sports Club *or*
b. **select a form** in common use by central or local government or your place of employment, and redesign it to make it easier to use.

4.5.4 Questionnaires

We do not devote much space to this matter, since good questionnaires are very difficult to design successfully. For example, it is easy to ask 'what kind of holidays do you prefer?', but very difficult to word a set of questions which will reveal why people prefer to go abroad for holidays, in a way which produces usable information. In principle, questionnaires are worth trying to design which seek the answers to very simple and straightforward questions: it is good practice to devise all of them so that the answers are always 'yes' or 'no'.

Form D — Confidential (Top)

MUNDY & NEWTON LTD
Eastfield Works,
Eastfield Road,
Southampton SO4 4PA

Telephone: (0123) 45678
Telex: 12345

APPLICATION FORM FOR APPRENTICES AND JUNIOR STAFF

Employment sought: Apprentice

Surname in block letters: WHITE
Forenames: Walter James

Home Address: 9b Grove Road, Eastleigh
Telephone No.: —

Place of birth: Dartford (?)
Nationality: British

Date of Birth: Day 22 Month Sept Year 61
National Insurance numbers (if any): —

How were you introduced to the firm? —

Full name and address of your father or guardian: as above

Full name and address of your family doctor: Dr. Morgan, Brockhane, Eastleigh

Please give details of any relatives employed by Mundy & Newton Ltd.: None

Have you suffered any serious illness or physical disability? If so, please give details: No

EDUCATION
Names and addresses of schools attended: Southleigh Comp.

Year and Month		Name of Head-teacher
From	To	Brooker
73	78	

EXAMINATIONS TAKEN

Subject	Year	Level	Grade
Mathematics	61		4
Tech Drawing	61		2

PREVIOUS EMPLOYMENT
Please give details of any employment you have had, including vacation work:

Name and address of employer	Description of work	From	To
Butlers Newsagent, Grove Road	Shop assistant (Saturdays)	May	July

INTERESTS
On the back of this form, please give details of your interests in and out of school e.g. sports, hobbies, positions of responsibility etc:

If you were offered employment, when would you be free to start? at the end of term

I certify that to the best of my knowledge the particulars given on this form are correct.
Signature of applicant: W.J. White   Date: July 14th
Signature of parent or guardian (for applicants under 18): ....

All candidates are required to be examined by the Works Medical Officer

---

Form D — Confidential (Bottom)

MUNDY & NEWTON LTD
Eastfield Works,
Eastfield Road,
Southampton SO4 4PA

Telephone: (0123) 45678
Telex: 12345

APPLICATION FORM FOR APPRENTICES AND JUNIOR STAFF

Employment sought: Apprentice Engineering Draughtsman

Surname in block letters: FORBES
Forenames: IAN JOHN

Home Address: 14 Grove Road, Eastleigh SO4 4BX
Telephone No.: None

Place of birth: Edinburgh
Nationality: British

Date of Birth: Day 14 Month 10 Year 1961
National Insurance numbers (if any): Not known

How were you introduced to the firm? School careers man

Full name and address of your father or guardian: Duncan Ian Forbes, 14 Grove Road, Eastleigh SO4 4BX

Full name and address of your family doctor: Dr W Morgan, N.3, 2 Fawcett Lane, Eastleigh SO4 4DL

Please give details of any relatives employed by Mundy & Newton Ltd.: None

Have you suffered any serious illness or physical disability? If so, please give details: Have been deaf in one ear since birth.

EDUCATION
Names and addresses of schools attended: Southleigh Comprehensive School, Warden Lane, Southleigh SO7 2DD

Year and Month		Name of Head-teacher
From	To	R.L. Brookes, M.A.
Sept 1973	June 1978	

EXAMINATIONS TAKEN

Subject	Year	Level	Grade
English	1978	CSE	2
Mathematics	"	CSE	1
Physics	"	CSE	2
Technical Drawing	"	GCE 'O'	C
Geography	1978	GCE 'O'	C
Woodwork	"	GCE 'O'	B

PREVIOUS EMPLOYMENT

Name and address of employer	Description of work	From	To	Reason for leaving
Queensway Ltd, Eastleigh Trading Estate, Eastleigh	Saturday storeman (furniture department)	Sept 1977	Now	Still employed

INTERESTS
On the back of this form, please give details of your interests in and out of school e.g. sports, hobbies, positions of responsibility etc:

If you were offered employment, when would you be free to start? 21st July 1978

I certify that to the best of my knowledge the particulars given on this form are correct.
Signature of applicant: Ian J. Forbes   Date: 14th April 1978
Signature of parent or guardian (for applicants under 18): D.I. Forbes

All candidates are required to be examined by the Works Medical Officer

> **Activity 33**
>
> **Devise a questionnaire** to the members of the sports club designed to find out whether the club bar should open on Sundays, and if so for how long – but in such a way that all the answers can be 'yes' or 'no'.

4.6 Pictorial representation

Information can be conveyed by many ways other than words and sentences. This section deals with the more important visual and pictorial means available.

4.6.1 Symbol and Logo

A *symbol* is a substitute for the thing or idea which it symbolises. A set of initials may come to serve as a symbol if it becomes well enough known. A set of letters in a distinctive type may do this quite quickly, and advertisers set out to achieve this immediate association.

Logos of West Midlands County Council and Shell U.K. Ltd and the British Standards Institution's 'Kitemark'.

But symbols need not consist of letters: most of the road signs in the Highway Code are example of this. Here too, the symbol may lie in the colour rather than the sign, as with the use of blue for motorway signs.

The term 'logo' has been coined to denote a visual symbol which identifies its bearer quickly and easily. The best examples are older than the word, but the use of skilled design has produced many more in recent years.

> **Activity 34**
>
> **Make a collection** of symbols and logos, discussing their 'meanings' and merits, with a view to devising a new one for, e.g. your local police force or a specialised unit of the armed services.

4.6.2 Charts

The main types of chart are known as pie-charts and bar-charts. Both are intended to be very easy to read, but the easier they are to use the harder they tend to be to produce.

A pie-chart seeks to show at a glance the way a given whole falls into its main parts. It therefore needs to say how big the whole is, and to avoid trying to go into detail. It is not a good way of displaying fine distinctions, or of showing the differences between parts of roughly equal size. Thus, Figure 1 shows clearly how a department store's employees are divided. Figure 2 shows only that the departments are of roughly equal size and if that were all that we wished to know there would be little point in producing such a chart. However it could be a useful device as, say, part of a series of pie-charts showing several different aspects of the firm and it could give a useful basis for making comparisons. See Activity 36a.

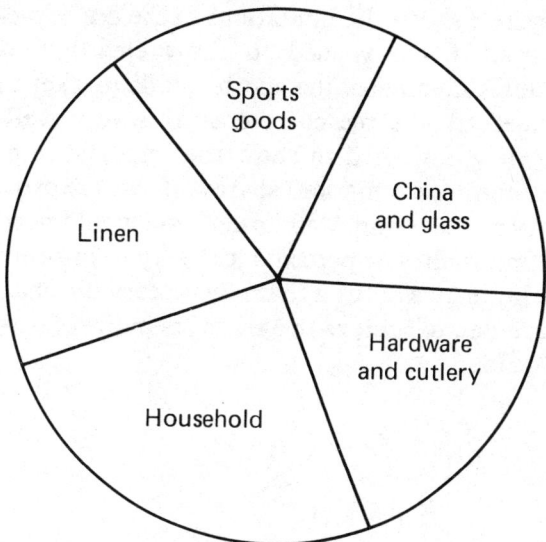

Riddles Ltd—distribution of departmental floor areas

Figure 2

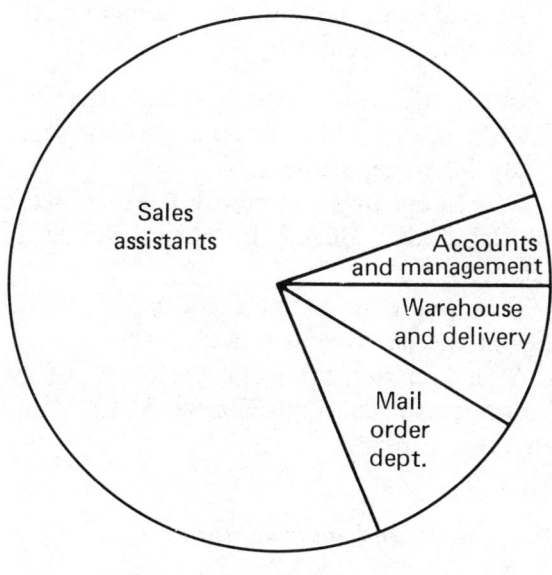

Riddles Ltd—distribution of 292 employees (1978)

Figure 1

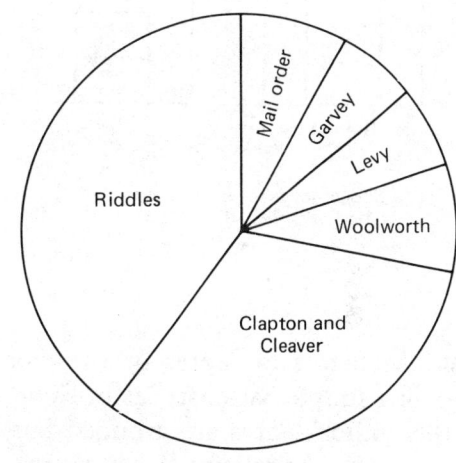

Sports goods—Lemeford area Market shares 1977-8 (est)

Figure 3

Activity 35

Discuss in class in what circumstances and by whom a pie-chart such as that in Figure 3 might be used.

47

Figure 3 shows the limitations in the use of pie-charts. If you wished to show clearly that Riddles dominates the sports goods market in Lemeford, the pie chart does this very well. But if you wished to show the importance of the combined market shares of Woolworth, Garvey, Levy and Mail Order, you would need to find figures or percentages to try to improve their pie-chart, but if that is necessary the chart has failed to achieve the aim of being very easy to read.

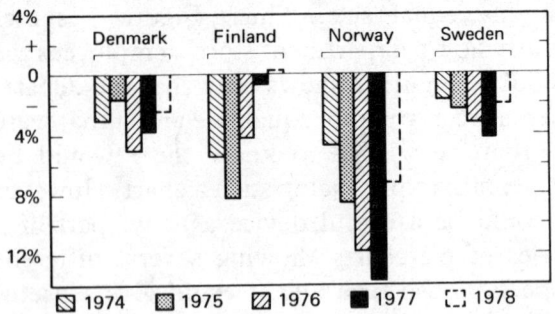

Figure 5

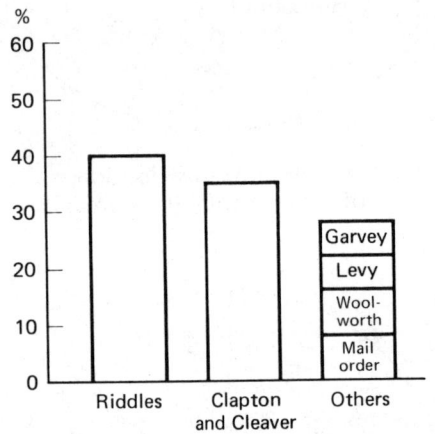

Figure 4

Activity 36

Explore in discussion, with close reference to the evidence, the truth or falsehood of the following statements:

a. Riddles Ltd run a sports goods department which is not as profitable a use of floor space as any other department.
b. It is likely that Clapton & Cleaver is the only specialist dealer in sports goods in Lemeford.
c. The best year for all Scandinavian countries in the last five years was 1978.
d. After Norway, the worst performer of the Scandinavian countries between 1974 and 1978 was Finland.

It would be better to represent the data of Figure 3 in a simple bar chart, as in Figure 4, where the 'minor' stores are grouped but the important point, the relative size of their combined share, emerges more clearly.

A bar-chart is much the most common form of pictorial representation of figures, but it can come in many guises. The bars can run horizontally or vertically. The bars can show positive and negative values – Figure 5 is an example where all four countries are shown as 'in the red'. This is, in fact, four separate bar-charts brought together.

4.6.3 Static and moving data

The pie-charts and bar-charts we have looked at so far have been concerned simply with presenting easily understood information in the clearest possible way, without any serious attempt to convey complicated or variable information. Figure 5 is the first chart in our series to show data of any complexity, by combining four separate bar-charts into one. Figure 6 shows the bar-charts greatest asset compared with the pie-chart: it can put items in order. The order may be one of size, as in Figure 6, or of time, as in Figure 7.

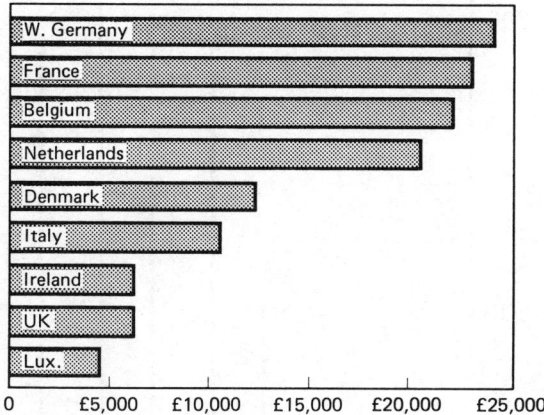

Figure 6 (May 1979 figures)

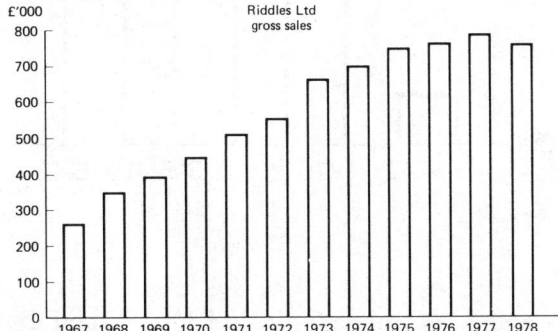

Figure 7

The temptation with any chart like Figure 7 or Figure 8 is to omit the bars and join up the ends to produce a 'graph'. This is wrong on two grounds. It suggests, firstly, that the data represented by one bar can change if the person or year moved towards the focus of another bar. For example, it might lead some readers to suppose that an MP in the UK could improve his financial position by moving to Belgium! The second objection is more serious: in Figure 8, it would suggest that the sales for, say, the second half of 1972 and the first half of 1973 were half way between the totals for each year — but the facts lying behind the chart give no basis for such a notion. Even so, a very large number of charts in business life, such as those of the share indices in the *Financial Times*, daily sales charts in production industries, and so on, are 'false graphs' of that kind.

Activity 37

Collect three or four examples of charts and graphs from newspapers and weekly journals, and analyse them to see how far the graphs are in reality bar-charts presented in graph form.

4.6.4 Comparability

Deaths from rheumatoid arthritis, County of x

1910–1930	145
1940–1950	133
1955–1960	146
1960–1962	154
1965–1967	221
1968–1973	481
1974–1977	218
1978	122

Figure 8

Consider the data given in the table in Figure 8. There are at least three serious objections to the table, which can be summed up in the generalisation that the figures given are not comparable with each other.

Activity 38

Discuss in class what objections could be offered to the table as presented in Figure 8. From the information given, **re-draw the table** so that the information is presented in a more acceptable form.

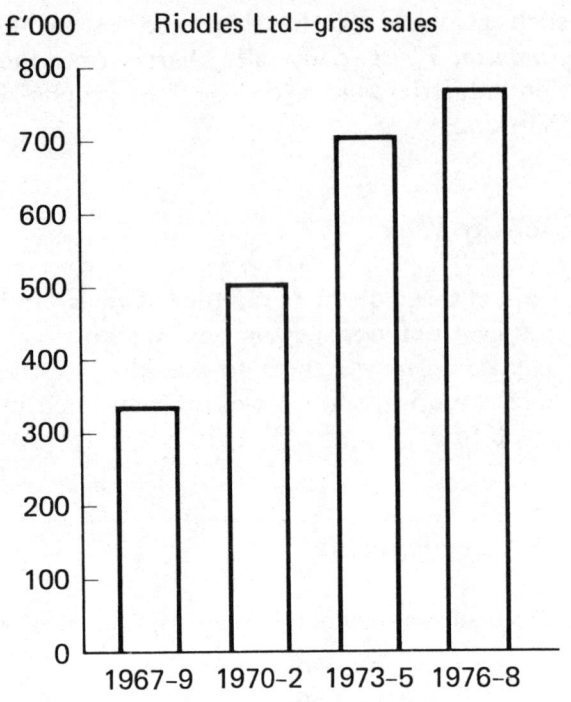

Figure 9

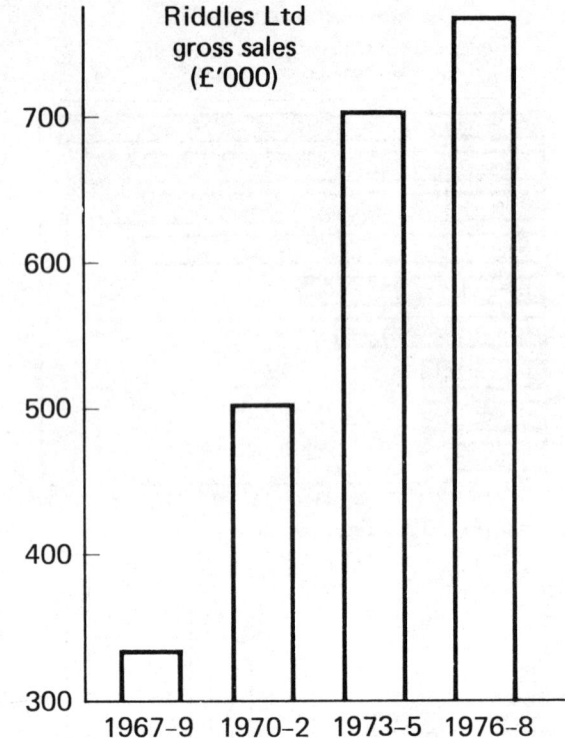

Figure 10

So far we have concentrated on ways in which information can be presented clearly and accurately by visual means. Visual presentation can be used to support a particular case which someone wishes to make. This is in fact a common use of graphs and charts. It is not necessarily dishonest, but it is certainly true that charts can be distorted to make a situation appear different from what it really is. The most common way of doing this is to change the base line in a bar-chart. If you compare Figures 9 and 10 they look very different, but if you consider them carefully you will see that they present exactly the same information and that the information is the same as that in Figure 7. The only real difference between Figure 9 and Figure 10 is that most of the height of some bars has been left out of Figure 10. Note also that Figure 10 does not start from 0 at the base line but from a figure of £300,000 and that each division of £100,000 in Figure 10 is given a wider space than in Figure 9. The effect of all this is to increase the apparent differences in Riddles' sales figures over the years shown.

Activity 39

Explore in discussion the reasons which a company treasurer might have for presenting the data of Figure 7 in the ways shown in Figure 9 or Figure 10.

The examples given in Figures 7–10 show that it is important, not only to notice whether figures are comparable, but also to note the small print, especially in the margin. Figure 11 is a particularly good example. At first glance,

50

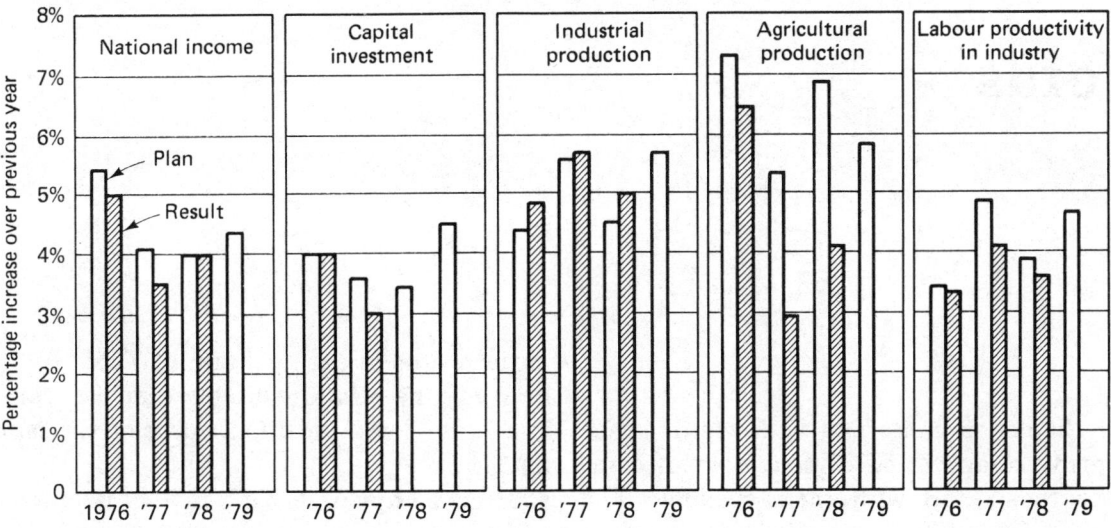

Figure 11

it suggests that Soviet national income is falling. If that were really the case, the chart would look very different. The explanation lies in the margins of the table. This set of bar-charts is worth detailed study because it provides many examples of the problems of interpreting visually presented information.

Activity 40

Explore in discussion, with close reference to the available evidence, the truth or otherwise of the following statements:

a. The growth in the sales of Riddles Ltd is tailing off and can be expected to cease altogether by 1980.
b. The rate of increase in deaths given in Figure 8 shows a steady rise over the whole period.
c. 1978 was an even worse year for Soviet planning than 1977.
d. In most countries the problem in 1976–78 has been to prevent economic activity declining. The Soviet economy seems to go on growing steadily all the time.
e. The least successful part of Soviet planning is agriculture.
f. Referring to current charges (as shown in *Post Office Guide* or the pamphlet *Postal Rates – Inland*) there is no satisfactory way of representing letter rates pictorially.

5 Words

5.1

This chapter is concerned with words, with the many complex and diverse ways of combining them, and with their spelling. The chapter will call for some close attention to detail about words themselves and the parts which make them up, about their structure, about the order in which they occur, and about the order and patterning of whole chunks of words. This attention to fine detail may be unfamiliar but it is essential: accuracy in the use of words is necessary for accuracy in the use of language.

5.1.1 The patterning of words

Table A

1.	2.	3.	4.
Certainty	Certain	Certainly	Ascertain
Circle	Circular	Circularly	Encircle
Clarity	Clear	Clearly	Clarify
Cohesion	Coherent	Coherently	Cohere
Conception	Conceivable	Conceivably	Conceive

Table B

1.	2.	3.	4.
	Decisive		
Depth			
			Deride
		Differently	
Digestion			

Activity 41

a. **Work out in discussion** what is common to the words in each column of Table A.
b. **Study the relationship** between the words in column 4 and the other words on the same line.
c. **Make a copy** of Table B in your notebook, and using the one entry on each line as a clue, fill in the blanks in the Table on the same model as Table A.

Activity 42

1. **Find several words** with each of the following endings and decide which column each word would belong in: -ity, -al, -ial, ful, -fully, -ise, -ate, ism.
2. **Explore in discussion** what precisely these word-endings mean.
3. **Select** any four of these word endings and make as long a list as possible of words which use them.

Activity 43

Repeat the work of Activity 42 for four other word-endings.

5.1.2 Words and affixes

The Tables in 5.1.1 can be repeated many times. You will notice that A and B use words from only one letter heading of the dictionary, and most other letter headings would provide a similar store of words. You will notice also that most of the differences between the columns occur at the ends of the words. One or two of them occur at the beginning. This pattern is a very common one in English, and is known as *affixation*.

Here is a simple table which gives examples of the pattern:

Table C

Prefix	Stem	Suffix
en-	-circle-	-ment
un-	-predict-	-able
dis-	-function-	-al
re-	-produc-	-tive
trans-	-port-	-ed

Activity 44

Copy this table into your notebook and find three other words which give you examples of a prefix, a stem and a suffix.

Activity 45

Find five further suffixes, giving two or three examples of words which use them, and work out what each suffix means.

Activity 46

Repeat this Activity with prefixes instead of suffixes.

'Predict' plus '-able' yields 'predictable'. This is related to 'predictability'. Such a word is an example of the pattern stem + suffix + suffix. This pattern occurs quite frequently in English and can be found in some words already used in this chapter.

Activity 47

Work out how many times in this chapter so far the pattern stem + suffix + suffix has occurred.

'Interchangeable' = 'inter-' + 'change' + '-able' = prefix + stem + suffix. 'Semi-interchangeable' = prefix + prefix + stem + suffix. This pattern is associated with technical writing.

Activity 48

Here are five prefixes: **say what each one means** and find five further examples of each:
semi as in semi-detached
post as in post-dated
para as in para-military
bi as in bi-valve
milli as in millipede

5.1.3 Gender — the unequal sexes

The treatment of male and female in English, as many feminists have observed, is not equal. Some words have a male or masculine version only, such as 'dog' or 'friar'. Some have a female or feminine only, such as 'daughter' or 'hind'. Some words come in closely related gender-pairs, such as 'hero/heroine' or 'actor/actress'. Most nouns (see below) which denote the sex of what they name have either a close pair or a well-known partner, such as 'sir/madam', 'boar/sow', 'gander/goose'. But there are some words which have no pair. Consider this pattern: 'Bus conductor/conductress' . . . 'Bus driver . . .?'

Activity 49

For each of the following, **give the pair or partner** word or the form of the word which would be used for the opposite sex.

a. Heiress, negress, duchess, governess, sorceress.
b. Author, proprietor, widower, lion, vixen.
c. Witch, sister, aunt, mare, men.
d. Masseur, executrix, Boy Scout, marquis, bride.
e. Frances, Lesley, Robert, Joseph, Cecilia.

5.2. Assembled words

5.2.1 Derived forms

If we were to draw on all the possible prefixes and suffixes for the purpose of making as many words as possible out of the component parts of a word-family, we would find the number sometimes very large. Here is a set of the component parts which can be attached to a single stem, and you will no doubt think of others:

Prefix	Stem	Suffix
ex-		-er
im-		-ant
un-		-ance
	-port-	-age
re-		-ing
mis-		-ed

In this example as in many others it is possible to use more than one prefix and more than one suffix, as in the word 'unimportantly'.

Activity 50

Find another example of the same pattern, setting out the stem and a range of possible prefixes and suffixes.

Some combinations of prefixes and suffixes are possible and others are not allowable: for example, 'exporter' is permissible and so is 'importance', but not 'exportance'.* (Note: exportance.* The * symbol marks a word which does not exist or a spelling mistake.)

5.2.2 Stress

There are differences between two forms of the same word which can be heard quite clearly in speech, and which can usually be understood in writing. Thus *im*port is a noun and im*port* is a verb.

Activity 51

Explore how stress and meaning go together in the two meanings of these words:

fragment
desert
incline
rebel
reject

5.2.3 Combination

Some words in English are the result of a repeated process of affixation, and one reason why students find 'long words' difficult is that they have not grasped how this process has developed. Here are some examples:

1. *Rebel* has the related adjective *rebellious* which can be turned into a noun as *rebelliousness*.
2. *Person* has the related adjective *personal* which can be turned into a related verb form *personalise* and has a negative in *depersonalise*.
3. *Employ* has a related adjective *employable*, which has given rise to the noun *employability*, and its negative form *unemployability*.

While it may not help in the short run to know how words like this are built up, sustained attention to it as you read will certainly lessen your need to refer to dictionaries.

Activity 52

a. For each of the following words **set out the**

component parts as has been done in the previous paragraph, noting if possible the order in which the components have been added:

counterproductiveness
humanitarianism
misrepresentation

b. **Build combinations** of three or four elements into words in the same way using the following stems:

bank
commune
stable
claim
profit
suppose

5.2.4 Compounding

Many English words are formed simply by joining other words end-on to them. Examples of this include: cocktail, firework, swimsuit, and sandpaper. In other cases compounds are formed by double words such as corn-meal, and car-port. (Whether these should have hyphens or not is a very difficult question. When in doubt use separate words without a hyphen unless you can find a one word form or hyphenated form in a dictionary.)

Activity 53

Find ten compound words which bring two separate words together to form a new word.

5.2.5 Word families and spelling

One of the benefits of studying the family relationships between words is that it will make a positive contribution to your spelling. For example, if you understand that *business* is the product of busy + ness, you are less likely to spell it on the false model of *building*. The same holds if you recognise a common element between con + fess = confess and pro + fess = profess/professor/profession. (In practice a great many errors like proffessor* arise from the doubling of a consonant in a word where another consonant is doubled. See below, section 5.6.4.)

A particular pattern can be observed in the relationships between members of particular word families. In the following table, the correct spelling of the word which fills the blank can be worked out with the help of the word supplied. The key feature which provides the help is where the stress falls.

Activity 54

Complete the following table and work out what all ten examples have in common:

adjective	*noun or verb*
grammatical	
dictatorial	
	analyse
finite	
	repetition
existential	
	familiarity
	competition
differential	
decisive	

5.3 Organising meanings

This conversation occurred at the site-hut on a building site, between a well-dressed visitor and three labourers:

'Johnson here?'
'Which one? Joe Johnson or Gaffer Johnson?'
'Gaffer, I suppose.'
'Ah! Gaffer Tom or Gaffer Tony?'
'Er . . . Tony, I think.'
'Right, now. Would you be wantin' Tony Stores or Tony Wages?'

'Oh, I see. Stores.'
'Thought so. Too bad.'
'Oh, why?'
'Well, he left. Two weeks back.'
'And you got another Johnson in his place . . .'

The information conveyed in this conversation would be organised very differently if it were written down: Mr Anthony Johnson, former Wages Manager. This sounds very simple and obvious, but the principle involved is important and explains a great deal of technical language. What is happening is that in conversation we grasp one fact and another is tacked to it, followed in turn by others. At each step a choice has to be made – in this example, between gaffer and non-gaffer, between Tom and Tony, between Stores and Wages. These choices are usually between sets of two or three choices at most. In writing we tend to get, not the process of making the choice one by one, but the complete outcome of the whole set – and the bits of information often come out in the reverse order, as in *Mr Anthony Johnson* (instead of Johnson . . . Tony . . .), and in *former Wages Manager* (instead of Johnson . . . gaffer . . . wages . . . left . . .). Where spoken language often provides information by adding on to the right, writing often adds to the left. Most writing, of course, does both, and has a third way of organising meaning which we shall call insertion.

5.3.1 Adding to the right.

Here is a sequence of headlines which could have appeared in a local newspaper at intervals:

Bus crash
Bus crash death
Bus crash death probe

and so on until this version:

Bus crash death probe bid rejection

A pattern like this can be extended a long way.

Activity 55

Select a simple headline and invent rightward additions which would tell a compressed story in the same way as the example just given.

5.3.2 Adding to the left

This example is taken from the sports page of a national newspaper in 1978.

> match
> much postponed match
> eagerly awaited but much postponed match
> important, eagerly awaited but much postponed match
> This tense, important, eagerly awaited but much postponed match

This pattern is much more common than adding to the right, because it is the basis of a great deal of informational and technical writing: these instances occurred in the weekly magazines of a typical week of 1978:

travel-variable Meyer-type cut-off valves
this very serious impending microelectronics crisis
dioxyribonucleic acid
electronic random number indicator
the Manpower Services Commission's job-creation and stimulus schemes

The point about this pattern of organizing meaning is that in order both to read them with understanding and to write them easily you have to be able to handle them as complete units.

Activity 56

From the textbooks in use for other subjects of your current course, **select a number of examples** of left-addition phrases like those quoted in 5.3.2, and explore their meanings in detail.

5.3.3 Insertions

There are some words in English which affect the meaning of what we say or write, but which affect it according to precisely where we put them. The next Activity explores this in detail. The one after that explores the related problem of expressions which convey more meanings than the writer intends.

Activity 57

Here are two sentences:

He found out the facts for himself
She makes occasional mistakes in her English

Explore with each of the following words the different positions in which they can (or cannot) be put into these two sentences, and examine the different shades of meaning which arise:

just	only
merely	quite
almost	rather
always	still

*   *   *

Activity 58

Explore the reasons for the ambiguities in these notices and discuss how they could be improved:

```
We dispense with care

His hair needs cutting badly

Dogs must be carried

SLOW MUD ON ROAD

HEAVY PLANT CROSSING

Flying aircraft can be dangerous

Nurses must not use the ground floor in
their pyjamas
```

5.4 Meaning and word-order

Many but not all the problems of unclear meanings arise from careless choices of words, but others arise from uncertainty about where to put them in order. In practice, the great majority of word-order problems arise from the kind of words dealt with in Activity 57. The next two Activities are designed to show you just how much you know about the word-order rules of English. Here is a selection of typical English phrases from good business writing, arranged so that the patterns of word-order in them show up more clearly:

our	previous	expensive	TV and radio	advertising	campaign
these	latest	multi-purpose	two-speed	Black & Decker	hand-drills
this	firm's	usual	free	wage-negotiation	policy
our	many	damaging	unpredictable	production	stoppages
all	those	two dozen	over-priced	apple	trees

Activity 59

Set out a table of six columns and five lines like that just given, and fill in a long phrase of the same type on each line without using *of* or *and*. It is best to start with the last column, and the following entries for it may be useful: rifle, sewing machine, camera, record player.

Activity 60

Here are five more long phrases, in which one or more words may be in a position which feels 'wrong'. **Explore in small-group discussion** the rightness or otherwise of various alternative orderings.

all our advance-booking angry passengers
your seven-jewelled pocket antique watch
the store's new self-correcting stock-control
　　computerised system
our concealed usual security arrangements
an over-managed, under-paid, under-manned
　　and over-criticised department.

5.5 The one, the many, and the self

This section deals with the problems of impersonal forms and how to handle words for groups of individuals. The commonest error is either

'If a person wants to do something, you have to start . . .'

or

'The family are going on holiday . . '

In the first case, 'a person' suddenly switches to 'you', and the reader does not know whether he is reading a 'he' sentence or a 'you' sentence. In the second case, 'the family' is singular but 'are' is plural, and the reader is unsure whether he is reading an 'it' sentence or a 'they' sentence.

5.5.1 One or many?

Do we say 'The family is going for a holiday'? 'The family', it might be thought, is several people and therefore plural. Consider other cases of nouns covering several people:

An army marches on its stomach
The club cricket team lost its first match.

Words like club, team, army, family, group, clutch, etc., are known as *collectives*. (Inventing new collective nouns is a well-known game – a scribble of authors, a suit of managers.) Collective nouns label groups and are always singular. This applies to several words which can work as collectives and in other ways: group, team, workforce, squad, the management, the company, number. These examples include four errors followed by four correct forms:

A squad of police were investigating the matter
Eleven men ought to make a team which work together
A bunch of fifteen rugby players usually are noisy in the evenings
The jury are returning
A battalion of six hundred soldiers is not fed by magic
The management is unable to agree to the whole claim
Such a large number is impossible to accommodate
My force of bricklayers is easily able to do that job.

5.5.2 A changing pattern

This general rule is giving way to one change which many older people regret: it is a good example of language changing in a way which causes disagreement. Phrases like 'A group of' and 'A number of' used always to be treated as singular:

A number of my staff feels unable to accept the idea

I have a group of students which is always hardworking.

In practice this has come to seem very formal and niggling to most people, for whom the verb (feels, is) should match the noun nearest to it, thus:

A number of my staff feel unable to accept the idea

I have a group of students who are always hardworking.

In general, if the plural item (staff, students) comes after 'a group of' or 'a number of' or a similar phrase, the sentence becomes plural:

A large number of teachers believe this to be acceptable.

5.5.3 Me, myself, and I

The '-self' forms are quite straightforward:

	singular	plural
I-form	myself	ourselves
you-form	yourself	yourselves
he-form	himself / herself / itself / oneself	themselves

There are no correct forms 'theirselves' or 'one's self'.

It is considered poor style to use *I* and *myself*, *he* and *himself*, etc in the same phrase:

He himself did not like the idea

is better written, if the emphatic form is essential, as:

He did not like the idea himself

and better still as:

He did not like the idea.

5.5.4 Person and company

One may have been taught at school that it is always wrong to write 'I' in essays. One may have found this a nuisance. One may suspect that the rule imposed at school does not apply in business English, and the preceding sentences of this paragraph illustrate why: 'one' is a clumsy way of putting it. There is no general ban on 'I', but business usage has to be careful, because a letter written by an individual employee on the firm's paper will commit the firm unless the letter makes absolutely clear that he is writing as an individual. This is the legal basis for many house-rules which forbid the use of 'I', but such a rule is the cause of much very bad writing.
For example:

```
We thank you for your enquiry addressed to
the undersigned concerning delivery dates
for carpeting of the Hawk brand.  The present
writer has made extensive enquiries and is
pleased to declare himself satisfied that the
supplier's assurances previously quoted are
reliable.
```

Now, it is tempting to suggest that the salesman write more simply, thus:

```
Thank you for your telephone call asking
about delivery of Hawk carpeting.  I have
investigated the quoted dates and am sure
they are reliable.
```

However, a company's liability for undertakings of a business nature may include meeting the financial losses incurred by those who rely on the undertakings and are let down. In that case, the letters in question have to make clear that they are written for and on behalf of the firm, and not by an employee in his own name. The matter of financial responsibility in law is a serious one, and lies behind much very formal writing in business correspondence, but most of this goes too far. In such a case, the salesman is fully 'covered' by writing:

```
Thank you for your telephone inquiry about
delivery dates quoted by this firm for Hawk
carpeting.  After further inquiry we are
able to confirm that the supplier's dates
are usually reliable.
```

5.5.5 *One*

It does not help to resolve the problem of legal liability to write 'One can take it that . . .' There are rare occasions when a writer cannot say 'I' or 'We' or 'he' but has no name to use instead, and on such occasions 'one' is very useful. But it is a trap for the unwary. Some uses sound painfully snobbish:

'One simply doesn't know what one will see nowadays, does one!'

But in trying to be gentle about giving orders it is possible to make matters even worse:

'One doesn't want to throw water all over the girls, do we.'

And if one is going to use 'one', it is essential that one sticks with it, unlike this:

The library has banned book-bags, and while one may not like it there is nothing whatever we can do about it.

In continuous writing of any kind likely to arise in this book, it is better to find another way round the problem, as here:

One does not like homework, but one does it and has it marked, and does the next lot. One goes on in a sort of routine, but then some of it is handed back unmarked, and that rather discourages you.

Better to use another route to the same end:

Homework is a routine, although not very likeable, and becomes a habit. What makes it difficult to keep up the habit is having it handed back unmarked.

The clumsy use of 'one' usually arises from attempts to convey a message too briefly, and the same general principle holds for improper uses of -self forms and confusions between singular and plural.

Activity 61

Discuss other ways of wording the following:

a. Employees should not park their motor-cycle or bicycle in the car park.
b. The company's policy towards their employees is unchanged.
c. A man deserves to succeed if they push theirselves that hard.
d. I'm very keen on badminton and my club are even keener.
e. It is forbidden for any employee to eat their lunch at a desk.

5.5.6 *His or her*

One of the most awkward language problems in business arises from the fact that we have no gender-neutral term to cover *him* and *her* and their relatives. This problem is not solved by such usage as letters which begin 'Dear Sir/Madam' or 'Dear Sir or Madam' (of which pair the second is the less unpleasant). It is partially solved by switching into the plural and writing 'Dear Sirs' *correct*. There is no plural form for Madam. It is probably better to find a function-label, as in 'Dear Ratepayer' or 'Dear Colleague'.

What, then, is to be done about problems like this:

Each member should bring his or her partner to meet the Chairman and should accompany him or her to dinner . . .

The general answer is to decide firmly which sex is in the majority in the relevant circumstances and use the one form only. It will sometimes be possible to find another way round, thus:

Each partner should be brought by the member to meet the Chairman and accompanied to dinner . . .

but such devices can become very stiff. If you do have to use the him/her solution, try to minimise the frequency of its occurrence. What is never correct is to submerge *him/her* in *them* or '*his or her*' in '*their*', treating the singular as the plural.

5.6 Spelling

It is not possible in the space available in a short book to provide a complete solution to the problems of spelling. We shall try to do two things: to show that different kinds of mis-spellings have different origins, and to show that most common mis-spellings can be corrected because the correct spellings are based on regular patterns.

5.6.1 Spelling is visual

Spelling has little to do with sound in the strict sense. For example, the final *s* on *boots* and that on *buzzers* are the same letter, but the sound is different. Again, we shall never learn to spell *peculiar* correctly by relying on sound, because there is no element of *a* sound in the word as we usually speak it. (We are much more likely to learn it by linking it with peculi*a*rity: see 5.2.5.) Spelling is a feature of the written language, and it therefore needs to be mastered as something visual: nine misspellings out of ten result not from careless speech or from dialect, but from careless *looking*. And the language encourages very rapid looking: we do not in fact look at every letter when we read, and we do not need to. This is obvious as soon's y'try rdng a v. cut or abbrevtd pce of Engl: but the habit of not looking closely when we read can easily become the same habit when we write.

5.6.2 Learning to spell

There are several steps in learning the written language. The very first (known to many as the 'phonics' stage) covered letters, especially the complex vowels. Students who still write words like *thier, beuty, gentul, metings* have been doing this since the infant school. There is a second stage, to do with word structures, much of which we have dealt with above under affixation, and examples of the misspellings that arise here include

disapear	sucesful
dissappearence	successfull
saftey	pursuade
unecessary	ilitterate
completley	carless

> **Activity 62**
>
> **Correct the spelling** of the ten words given above.

5.6.3 Using the spelling system

In practice, students who have left school (and who are not seriously behind in their reading as well as writing) make three main kinds of spelling mistake. The errors in this sentence include these:

Some people go on typing the words, hopeing they are speling them alright and fussyly or busyly lookin up a few of them.

The three main kinds of mistake are:

1. Keeping in a final -e when it ought to be omitted on affixation
2. giving a double consonant as a single or vice-versa
3. failing to change a final y to an i on affixation.

Affixation here covers not only the addition of a suffix but the addition of such affixes as a final -s, -ed, -ing, -ly, etc.

Almost all instances of these three kinds of mistake occur in particular places. Consider these words:

towards
today
together
tomorrow
tomato

What have the first four in common that *tomato* lacks?
Breaking the words down, we find these structures:

   to
(back) + wards
= towards

to + gather
= together

   to
(yester) + day
= today

to + morrow
= tomorrow

but *not* to + mato

That is to say, the other four words contain a *junction*, but *tomato* does not.

5.6.4 Junctions

For the remainder of this section we will mark spelling errors with *.

We have met junctions before: in the matter of hyphens, and throughout the treatment of prefixes, stems, and suffixes earlier in this chapter. In order to explain how junctions affect spelling, we need to grasp two basic ideas. One is the distinction between Consonant and Vowel, which will become clear in a moment. The other is the idea of the suffix, which is set out in 5.1.1–3. Here we need to bring these two ideas together in order to distinguish two kinds of suffix:

A   -ing   -ed   -ive   -ial
as in: tracking rated   massive industrial

        -ity   -or   -ence   as in:
      cavity governor confidence

B   -s   -less   -ful   -ness
as in: hopes hopeless hopeful hopelessness

Type A suffixes begin with a vowel (a, e, i, o or u) while Type B begin with a consonant. (We shall use the symbol V for a vowel letter and C for a consonant letter.)

All junctions are made either by simple addition (cook+ing, to+day, etc.) or by making some minor change to the items which are joined.

Activity 63

Carry out the following by using junctions involving simple addition:

make an adjective from *dough, sloth, autumn, gnarl, joy*; make a negative of these by adding a prefix: *hopeful, appear, complete, fair, do.*

Change junctions I
The addition of a V-suffix (such as -ing, -ed,

ive, etc.) to a word ending -e must affect the spelling:

craze+ing	crazeing*	crazing
revise+er	reviseer*	reviser
dictate+or	dictateor*	dictator

In these cases, and others like them, the final e is deleted before a V-suffix.

Activity 64

Operate the rule that a V-suffix added to a final -e deletes the e in the following cases;

safe+er
analyse+is
please+ure
severe+ity
complete+ing
convene+or
cone+ical
revere+ence
precise+ion
type+ical

Find ten more examples of words ending in e to which V-suffixes may be joined in the same way.

Change junctions II
Any suffix added to a Y changes it to I **unless**

1. the suffix itself begins with i

or

2. the y follows a vowel

Thus:

happy+ness	happyness*	happiness
happy+er	happyer*	happier
merry+est	merryest*	merriest
carry+ed	carryed*	carried

But:

hurry+ing	hurrying
boy+ish	boyish
toy+s	toys

Activity 65

Operate the rule for Y-change given above in the following cases:

industry+ous
enjoy+able
delay+ed
destroy+ing
holy+er

quarry+es
fury+es
enjoy+ment
roly-poly+es
bury+ed

Change junctions III
Many suffixes are joined to stems which end in a consonant, but knowing when to double the C is often a problem: sit+ing = sitting, but brim+ful = brimful. The rule is in fact fairly simple, but see first if you can work it out from these examples.

Activity 66

By adding -ing or -er to the following, try to **identify** the features in the stem which lead to C-doubling on affixation:

swim	grab	treat	trip	grasp
strain	scrub	crown	upset	distract

The suffix has the effect of doubling the preceding C

a. if it is itself a V-suffix

and

b. the letter before the double C is a V, and the

Letter before that is a C. i.e. the pattern is CVC + V-suffix.

Thus

sit+ing	= CVC + V-suffix	sitting
big+er	= CVC + V-suffix	bigger
time+ing	= VCV + V-suffix	timing
tin+ing	= CVC + V-suffix	tinning
dine+ing	= VCV + V-suffix	dining
dine+er	= VCV + V-suffix	diner
scornful+ful	= C-suffix	scornful

(Note that in *dinner* there is no junction.)

Activity 67

Make a list in your file of all the suffixes used in Section 6.5 thus far. Select twenty stems used as examples in the same section, and join to each of them a suffix not already used with it in this section.

5.6.5 I before E

The well-known rule about 'i before e except after c' is only well-known in its incomplete form: the full version of it reads, 'i before e except when, after c, the sound is *ee*'. This will account for amost all the apparent exceptions to the rule, which are exceptions only to the incomplete form of it.

5.6.6 A list

The following items are listed for learning separately because they are very common and have not been specifically covered in the previous notes.

broad (adj) breadth (n)
breath (n) breathe (vb)
compara*t*ive/superla*t*ive
con+science = conscience/conscious/conscientious
con+venient = convenient/convenience

despair/desp*e*rate/desp*e*ration
develop (not develope) but envelop (vb)
envelope (n)
licence (n) license (vb) licensee
practice (n) practise (vb)
practitioner
prophecy (n) prophesy (vb)
prophet
mischief/mischievous (not mischievious*);
so also grievous
occur/occurred/occurrence
recur/recurred/recurrent
privilege
psychology
pursue/pursuit
prefer/preferred/preference/preferential
refer/referred/reference/referential
seize/seizure
separate/separation/reparation
sheriff
siege
subtle/subtlety/subtly
symmetry/symmetrical

Activity 68

Learn the items listed above.

5.6.7 General

We have dealt with the three most common problems with spelling among students who have left school, but there are others. The most useful general advice to give is this: if you work through all the Activities in this book you will gradually develop a new kind of attention to the details of words, and that is in the long run your best hope. If you insist on believing that spelling is not important, we cannot help you. The first step to good spelling is to *want* to do it. If your schooling has given you the mistaken belief that your employers will not be bothered about spelling, you will find it a problem until your underlying attitude changes. If you want to improve it, however, these exercises are not enough: you will also need a sustained and wide exposure to written English. It does not much matter whether this takes the form of reading a 'posh' paper daily or every Sunday, or of having a sustained read through the works of any novelist from Ian Fleming or Morris West or Alan Sillitoe to Dickens or Dostoevski. The point is that this deep and long taking-in of written language is painless, and is teaching you about the writing system of English more effectively than all the classwork and exercises ever invented.

6 Punctuation

6.1 Why is punctuation a problem?

There are two answers to this question. One is that teachers vary in their treatment of it. At one extreme it is treated as a set of rigid rules which must always be observed. At the other extreme it is regarded as a minor nuisance which can be learned when you need it. Most teachers fall somewhere in between.

The other answer is that the rules which govern the working of the punctuation system are indeed very complicated. Recent studies have made the rules better understood but although we base our account here on this recent work, we have tried to present a simple, practical guide to punctuation. Some punctuation does conform to rigid rules but much of it does not.

6.1.2 Is punctuation important in business life?

Yes. Communication is the conveying of meanings, and the punctuation system is one of the ways of doing just that. Consider this fragment of a note about an awkward negotiation:

> Chairman nodded at me and Davies seeing this left the room

Did Davies leave because he saw the nod? Because the chairman nodded at both of them? The absence of three commas confuses the reader and obscures the meaning. Multiply this kind of problem thousands of times, and you will see that punctuation can and does matter. Many employers, too, expect 'educated' people to be able to punctuate – especially if they cannot do it themselves.

6.1.3 What punctuation does and does not do

It does three things:

1. it separates units which come one after another so that we can see they are separate. (A 'unit' can be a word, a group of words, or something much longer.)
2. it separates units which are 'tucked inside' (or included in) other units (see 6.8 below).
3. it identifies some things, which can have several meanings, as having one particular meaning.

On the other hand,

4. it does *not* act as mere decoration, to be put in afterwards
5. it does *not* act as a complete version of how something is spoken
6. it is *not* a matter of personal fancy.

6.1.4 How does punctuation do the separating and identifying?

1. Separating successive units is done by:

paragraph spacing ⎫
space between sentences ⎬ See 6.3
space between words ⎪
the hyphen ⎭

full stop ⎫
single comma ⎬ 6.5
colon   6.6
semi-colon 6.7

2. Separating the 'tucked in' or *included units* is done by

brackets ⎫
paired dashes ⎬ See 6.8
paired commas ⎪
quotation marks ⎭

3. Identifying specific meanings is done by

capital letters   6.3
single dashes ⎫
solidus or oblique stroke ⎪
some layout conventions ⎬ See 6.9
abbreviation marks ⎪
apostrophe ⎭

6.1.5

We shall deal with punctuation in the order given in the preceding paragraph. Those who need to investigate further should study Carey's *Mind the Stop*, while specialists will find a detailed technical account, to which we are much indebted, in Quirk et al – *Grammar of Contemporary English*, Appendix III.

6.2 Punctuation and pauses

Many treatments of punctuation in English have tried to relate it to pauses in speech. This is a good example of the 'rigid rules' approach, because it does not fit the facts. Many stops occur in written text which correspond to no pauses whatever when the text is read aloud. Many pauses in speech have no punctuation in writing. The length of the pauses does not, in fact, vary according to the weight of the stop. For example, this paragraph could be read aloud with or without pauses at the commas.

6.2.1

Punctuation in written English is governed partly by the grammatical structure of what is written. We do not attempt in this book to provide the grammar involved, because it is very complex. Our examples and our arrangement of the material rely on our knowledge of grammar, but you do not need to know the grammar in order to understand them.

6.2.2

However, there are some features of speech which do relate to some parts of the punctuation system. These are less often pauses than changes in pitch. Consider this sentence:

> The chairman was not willing, partly because of the committee's constitution, to carry out the business with only four members present.

There the first comma marks a change in pitch (if the sentence were spoken aloud) and the second marks a return to the pitch of 'was not willing'.

6.3 Punctuation as a separating system

6.3.1

Written English marks the boundaries between paragraphs in three ways:

1. the last sentence of a paragraph need not fill the line.
2. the next paragraph begins on a new line, and in print there will usually be a line-space as well.
3. the new paragraph begins with an indent

(i.e. the first word starts some spaces in from the left margin). The normal indent is about 1 centimetre, but in text using sub-headings need not be used.

6.3.2

The boundary between sentences is also marked in three ways:

1. a full stop at the end of a sentence
2. a capital letter at the beginning of the next sentence
3. a space between them equivalent to twice the normal space between words.

6.3.3

The space between words may seem a very obvious matter, but some students write with too small or too large a word-space, and either habit makes their writing needlessly difficult to read. The normal word-space is the same size as the space needed for the letter *m*. (Printers have a technical term, an 'em', and measure spaces as equivalent to so many ems.)

6.3.4

The word-space in English is important because writing has to distinguish between strings of words which in speech can (and do) sound alike but can be understood from context: compare *a nice drink* with *an iced drink*. But there are three ways of treating the word space, and it is often hard to choose between them. Consider:

| tax payer | tax-payer | taxpayer |
| yard rule | yard-rule | yardrule |

That is to say, the word space can be observed, omitted, or bridged with a hyphen. Historically, hyphens often link two words which were once separate but are on their way to becoming single words (like *taxpayer* above).

Words which have completed this process include longhand, shorthand, workforce. Words which are probably in the middle of the process include pop-star, space-man, oil-fired. The only advice we can give here is to use a recent dictionary and consult your teacher.

6.3.5

There are three special cases of the hyphen to note:

1. some phrases are written as separate words but when used before a noun become hyphenated:

You'll have to do it yourself.
A do-it-yourself shop.
His work is always well produced.
His well-produced work.

2. when two hyphenated items coming close together have the same second element, a special pattern occurs:

His work, however well-produced or ill-produced, always sells.
His work, however well- or ill-produced, always sells.

3. as an alternative to quotation marks:

He has taken up a 'blow you Jack, I'm all right' attitude.
He has taken up a blow-you-Jack-I'm-all-right attitude.

This is rightly criticised as journalistic. We disapprove of it unless and until you can write as fluently as a good journalist, because the quotation-mark method does just as well.

6.4 *The sentence stops*

The major stops are the comma, colon, semicolon, and full stop (known in American English as the period). Two variants of the full stop are the question mark or query and the exclamation mark.

6.4.1

The exclamation mark is very rare in business English. It is like the full stop in marking the end of a sentence, and is used to show that a statement or command is emphatic or stressed. See examples in 6.4.2. The question mark also operates like the full-stop in marking the end of a sentence, and applies to questions both emphatic and unemphatic.
Note the following:

1. There is no correct emphatic question form such as ?! or !??
2. if ? is used other than at the end of a sentence it should go in brackets showing an 'author's comment'.
3. for indirect questions, see para. 3.5.

6.4.2 There are thus six kinds of sentence in English:

	Unemphatic	Emphatic
Statement	My son arrived about noon	He got there!
Question	Did he reach home early?	He got here early?
Command	Please come on home now.	Get back at once!

It is a good general rule in business English that if you need to use an emphatic form you need to re-write the whole sentence.

6.5 Stops as messages

Every stop conveys a message to the reader. Each stop can convey one of several messages. The particular message depends on the writer's meaning. That meaning often depends on the situation. In our examples we have often simplified the situations to make them clearer. That means that the examples are over-simplified. We shall come back to this problem again.

6.5.1

The full stop signals that the writer has reached the end of a unit. Read paragraph 6.5 aloud, to a friend or into a tape-recorder. If you listen carefully, you will find that your voice has marked the end of each unit in a way which corresponds to the full stops. There are no punctuation marks in speech, of course, but there are changes in pitch, which punctuation often reflects, but the match between the two is never exact. The next activity explores this.

Activity 69

Re-write paragraph 6.5
a. as three sentences
b. as two sentences
c. as one sentence.
Then one student should read out his versions of (a) and (b) while the others identify where the full stops occur.

6.5.2

The comma is the obvious stop to deal with next, partly because it is by far the most common of the stops, partly because it is rather complicated, and therefore causes many problems, so we have divided its complexities up, and will take them in separate stages.

Activity 70

a. **Read the preceding paragraph (6.5.2) aloud** to a friend or into a tape-recorder. You may need two or three attempts to read the whole paragraph as one sentence (which it is). It is thus one unit, but it contains several sub-units: count these.
b. **Work out in discussion** how and where it could be divided into separate sentence units.

6.5.3

The lesson of Activity 69 is that the use of the comma and full stop may depend on how a writer wants to organise his meanings. They also depend on how the writer expects his text to be used: if you reconsider Activity 68, you will realise that one version is more suitable than another for silent reading, but a different punctuation would be more useful if the text is going to be read aloud.

6.5.4

The central feature of the parts of a sentence which are separated by commas (rather than colons, semi-colons or full stops) is that they cannot stand as sentences on their own. There is no clear definition of a sentence which is both accurate and simple: definitions require a knowledge of grammar which we do not take for granted and do not think it necessary to include in this course. In any case, grammar is not the whole story: it is one way of organizing meanings, but punctuation provides writing with another. The two overlap, but are not the same. So it is better to work through a series of examples.

Activity 71

a. **Identify the items** in the following passage that could stand on their own as sentences. Each item is marked off by /. Different readers will treat some items differently. There is no 'one right way' to read such a passage.

there is history and history / as every reader knows / who has read *1066 and All That* / the Battle of Britain is a case in point / for over thirty years its anniversary has been celebrated on September 15th / based on a claim which has turned out to be quite untrue / British propaganda claimed at the time that on that day the RAF shot down 185 German Aircraft / after the war the records could be studied in great detail / when it became obvious that the claim was exaggerated / the real figure was certainly below 60 / according to the best authority / there has been a move to change the date to August 18 / when the total shot down was 69 / a figure higher than any other day in the authentic records / the difficulty with changing dates like this is public inertia / every kind of official calendar / thousands of diaries and reference books / even hundreds of thousands of school textbooks / give the later date as the key one / who is influential enough to change all that

b. Having done this, **decide how the items which cannot stand on their own as sentences are to be linked with those that can.** There are, of course, several acceptable solutions. You will find that each item which cannot stand on its own has to be associated with one that can, but also has to be separated from it by a comma. *The comma is a separation marker for items which have to be linked, through not being sentences or through being put into sentences with other items.*

(For other uses of the comma see 6.8 below.)

6.6 The Colon

The colon is much easier to deal with: it has only one message to convey. It is this: the words coming after a colon fill out what has come immediately before it. This very restricted meaning of the colon has one other consequence: it does not occur very often. Moreover all the sentences in this paragraph have a common feature: they are examples of how the colon should be used.

> **Activity 72**
>
> **Identify** in each sentence of 6.6 the word before the colon which is filled out or explained after it.

6.6.1

The 'colon and hyphen' (or :–) meaning 'as follows' thus tries to do the work of the colon twice over. Those who understand the proper use and meaning of the colon have no need of the extra hyphen or dash.

6.7 The Semi-colon

The semi-colon is more complicated than the colon. One reason for its difficulty is that it is relatively uncommon outside specialist or academic work. The simplest way to look at it is to regard it as the nearest punctuational substitute for *and*, more especially for *and* when it follows a comma. Another way to regard the semi-colon is as a bond between two items which could quite well stand as separate sentences, but which are more closely related than either of them is to the surrounding items. Here are some examples:

The war in the air over Britain in 1940 developed in two distinct phases. The first phase was a head-on effort to destroy the airfields from which the RAF operated. The second began when the German thrust was diverted to civilian targets; but even this was in due course frustrated, as the first thrust had been, by the RAF fighter squadrons. In both phases the attack came closer to success than the German leadership ever realised.

The Battle of Britain also illustrates another danger of popular history. Its tactics and strategy have been described in many books and articles as debates between leading characters like Dowding and Park. In reality these disputes would have arisen in any case; the arguments had very little to do with the personalities who took part in them; and the decisions would have been just as right or wrong if different people at the top had taken them. War is very rarely a matter of personal behaviour.

6.7.1

Another instance of the semi-colon to separate parts which hang together is its use in connected lists, to show the groupings in them:

> The RAF needed supplies of every kind: fighters, bombers, trainers, reconnaissance aircraft; bombs, ammunition, fuel, instruments, spares; pilots, navigators, gunners, maintenance men, flight controllers, cooks; buildings, land, administrative support, and above all secrecy.

6.7.2

The semi-colon and the colon can be confused in one usage:

> The government was prepared to use compulsion on all these necessities for the war in the air except one: aircrew had to be volunteers.

or

> . . . except one; namely, aircrew had to be volunteers.

The colon is appropriate if the explanation follows without an 'indicator' phrase such as *namely* or *this was*. When there is such an 'indicator', the semi-colon is used.

6.8 The punctuation of 'included units'

Consider this passage:

> Later on, after the development of airborne radar, an aircrew in a large aircraft (pilot,

navigator, engineer, observer, two or more gunners) could set out on a coastal patrol – or any other long flight – with some confidence that they would not be 'caught napping' or taken unawares by unseen enemy aircraft.

This passage uses all the punctuation marks for showing items which can be 'tucked in' during a sentence. The core sentence is quite simple:

> Later on the crew of a large aircraft could set out on a coastal patrol confident that they would not be taken unawares by enemy aircraft.

The inclusions put into this sentence are put in with different devices:

After the development of airborne radar
        is included with paired commas
(pilot, navigator . . . etc)
        is included in brackets
or any other long flight
        is included between dashes
caught napping
        is included in quotation marks.

Brackets and dashes are alternative versions to the paired comma and behave in very similar ways. We deal with paired commas in detail, but the same principle, that inclusions have an opening mark and a closing mark, always applies. This is obvious with the bracket (as you can see here if an opened bracket somehow is left unclosed. When we have dealt with paired commas you will be able to come back to look at brackets and dashes.

6.8.1 Inclusions in commas

Consider the following:

Dealing with inclusions is one of the commonest and most often misused ways of using the comma. Insertions in the middle of a sentence can be unexpectedly even surprisingly useful. These 'included items' as we have called them come in all shapes and sizes. They can be examples as this passage shows of a wide variety of meanings. There are also very few rules unfortunately about where in the sentence inclusions can come.

Now consider this version:

Dealing with inclusions is one of the commonest, and most often misused ways of using the comma. Insertions in the middle of a sentence can be unexpectedly, even surprisingly useful. These 'included items', as we have called them come in all shapes and sizes. They can be examples, as this passage shows of a wide variety of meanings. There are also very few rules, unfortunately about where in the sentence inclusions can come.

If you are not made very uncomfortable by the second version, you should be. The reason will be obvious to most readers: each inclusion is given its opening comma but not its closing one.

Activity 73

1. **Identify each inclusion** in the passage given in 6.8.
2. **Explore in discussion** whether any of them can acceptably come at other points in each sentence
   a. without any additional words
   b. with such words.

6.8.2 Inclusions and position

The inclusions we have looked at so far have all been placed in the middle of sentences, so that the comma on either side of each one is clearly visible. In practice a great many inclusions occur at the beginning or end of a sentence, with obvious consequences for the punctuation.

Activity 74

Consider the following:

By the later stages of the war the character of aircrew had changed or had become more varied. As everybody knew the fighter pilot was an individualist needing quick reflexes and great self-reliance a combination not always ready to accept discipline. When the aircraft changed radically the requirements of the crew changed too and changed more than some of the participants expected. When you put together crews of nine or twelve men you create a need for leadership and teamwork which ordinary fighter pilots could not know how to provide.

a. **Study the text** in order to identify the inclusions. There are at least two in each sentence.
b. **Explore in discussion** whether those coming at the start of a sentence could just as well have been placed later in it.
c. **Explore the possible positioning** of the inclusions placed at the end of any sentence.
d. **punctuate the sentences** appropriately.

6.8.3 Inclusions and pitch

It would be useful at this point, in view of the study given to the text in Activity 74, to listen to it read aloud, paying close attention to the speaker's pitch. Then do the same with the text studied in 6.8.1. Whether in the middle of a sentence or otherwise, each inclusion is given a slightly different pitch of the voice from that given to the main part of the sentence. When this happens in the middle of the sentence, the inclusion brings a slight rise or fall, and at the end of the inclusion the sentence goes on with the pitch as it was just before it.

This pattern is of considerable help in dealing with the problem of some 'which'-clauses:

The USAF became dependent on the radar system which the British had invented.

Whether or not to put a comma after *system* depends on a shade of meaning: if the sentence focus is on the USAF's dependence, the role of the British is a very minor consideration, there is no change of pitch after *system*, and no comma. If the focus is on the Britishness of the invention, the which-clause carries a main stress (on British or invented) and a comma is required.

Activity 75

Given below is a typescript written by a bored typist in a spare moment. Her spelling is good, but there are twenty errors to correct. Most of them are punctuation, but you will not correct all the errors solely by changing the punctuation.

```
Dear Jane -
Joes being thrown out of college, this
is a pity of course but Im not too
bothered for him.  My real worry is
about us, hell lose his grant as well
and we coul'nt live without that,
could we!  He saw the dean but even
though he had a terrific record in his
first year theres only a faint chance
of a rethink.  Can we come and talk to
your father please - He always was one
of Joes heroe's: ever since he showed
him a prof could be human.  Which he
didn't have to do ...
```

6.8.4 Lists

We deal with the comma as marker of grammatical structure in 6.5.2–6.5.4 and the comma as marker of inclusions in 6.8.1–6.8.3. It remains to deal with the only other use of the comma, which is to separate the items in a list. The items separated in this way can be words, numbers, phrases, or the parts of a natural sequence. The usual rule is that the last item in a list is preceded by *and* rather than a comma, but this is not obligatory.

'Thank you, sir. That will be £1.21p. Twenty-three, twenty-five, thirty, forty, fifty, two pounds. Three, four, five pounds.'

'Yes, I'd like three pounds of potatoes, please, a half of tomatoes, a lettuce, a cucumber, three lemons and a grapefruit.'

Detached hse, 3 recep, 4 bedr, bathrm, sep WC, dble gar, grnhse with WC, good garden.

Mrs Mary Gordon, Flat 2, 145 Hinton Lane, Clopting, NE88.

He has O Level passes in History, English, Maths, and CSE Grade 1 in Geography, Woodwork, Biology and Chemistry.

6.8.5 *Quotation marks*

There are examples of quotation marks in several preceding paragraphs. You will notice that none of these examples is a case of punctuating direct speech (which is referred to in another chapter). There is no difference between quotation marks and speech marks, for quotations and speech are both, basically, inclusions. Quotation marks use single inverted commas, and are used in citing the following:

1. short word-for-word extracts from other writing
2. titles of books, etc., where those are not in italics
3. words which are colloquial, slang, or improper
4. words which are being used in a special or odd meaning (such as technical terms which have just been introduced)

6.9 Specific meaning marks

capital letters:
1. To identify proper names.
2. To mark ordinary nouns as titles. (The first professor to speak was Professor Mayer).
3. As part of the marker of a new sentence or paragraph.

apostrophe: (see 6.9 below)

single dash:
1. Usually an alternative to the colon
2. Sometimes an alternative to the comma marking an end of sentence inclusion

emphasis marks:
1. Underlining (single words or short phrases only)
2. **Bold face**
3. The use for single words, in informal text, of CAPITALS

the solidus or oblique stroke:
also called 'slant' or 'slash', denotes subsectioning or, in dates, abbreviation: 1978/9 (alternative to 1978–9).

dates:
17th November 1979 can be written in several ways:

1. November 17 1979 is correct American usage
2. 17.11.79 is acceptable informal English (but see Addresses)
3. 17.xi.79 and xi/17/79 are acceptable American variants
4. 17/11/79 and 17–11–79 are acceptable in English usage only in informal settings.

addresses and letters:
(see Chapter 2 for full treatment).

abbreviations
are marked by the abbreviation mark (which is not the same as a full stop though it uses the same symbol). There are three general types of exception, where no abbreviation mark is expected:

1. where the abbreviated form ends with the final letter of the word:

Mr   Mrs   Dr   the Revd
and similar titles of all kinds have now followed suit:
Maj-Gen   Prof   Lt-Col MSc BA DSO
2. acronyms, i.e. strings of initials which have become words in their own right: UNESCO, USA, EEC, NASA.
3. a handful of widely used abbreviative expressions:
etc   no (for number)   ie   eg   a/c (for account)
In very formal text this group of expressions is avoided.

6.9.1 The Apostrophe

Apostrophes have three uses: to show omission of a syllable, to show omission of a letter, and to mark possession. Here are some examples:

Mary's coat wasn't on its peg, so she missed her 'bus.
    c   b   a

I can't see six weeks' work lost just for a 'phone call!
   b   c   a

My brothers' absence was due to 'flu: they'd both caught it.
      c   a   b

Activity 76

a. work out the common feature of the *a* type of apostrophe.
b. work out from the examples given the difference between the *b* and *c* types.

1. Syllable omission
Historically, words like omnibus, telephone, taxicab and influenza have had shortened forms. ('bus, 'phone, 'cab, 'flu.). The omitted syllable used to be shown by an apostrophe, but the marking has become almost extinct. It is now acceptable to write *bus*, *phone*, etc. without apostrophe.

2. Letter omission
This is the (*b*) type from our previous example:
don't for *do not*   *isn't* for *is not*
won't for *will not*   *can't* for *cannot*

Note the placement: other letters beside the o in *not* may be omitted, but the omission marked by the apostrophe is always n't. Thus, can't, never ca'nt,* wo'nt,* doe'nt,* etc. By extension of this practice, we find letter omission in

he's for *he is*
we've for *we have*
I'd for *I would* (sometimes written as *I'ld**)

These omissions occur singly: they should not be piled up on one another. Thus

he would not have done it
may become
he wouldn't have done it
or
he would not've done it
but not
he wouldn't't've done it*
and never
he wouldn't of done it!*

In formal writing this use of the apostrophe, for marking letter omission, is generally unacceptable.

3. To show possession
Almost always as *'s* rather than the apostrophe on its own.
   The basic rule is that the apostrophe for

possession has a following *s* always, unless there is an *s* already in front of it (and sometimes even then).

1. in ordinary singular nouns

Mr Sharp's car	my friend Jennifer's handbag
a good day's work	a year's work wasted

2. in plural nouns which do not end in *s*: compare these two columns:

one man's meat	two other men's poison
one woman's magazine	the women's magazines
a sheep's clothing	fifty sheep's bleating
a child's toy	children's games

3. in nouns which end in *s* or *ss*, whether singular or plural. Here the *s* is not usually repeated in the written form, though it is sometimes spoken.
Compare these two columns:

a lady's hat	two ladies' cardigans
the mistress's wishes	the mistresses' concern
the year's work wasted	ten years' work wasted
in one week's time	three weeks' holiday

One of the few exceptions is the London street: St James's. Note that dresses, princesses, etc are ordinary plurals, not possessives at all. Their possessive form is rare, thus:

the stresses' main cause (better to write 'the main cause of . . .')

6.9.2 *Some advice*

The apostrophe always makes students anxious. Because it is the omission of the apostrophe that teachers tend to mark as wrong, the temptation is to resolve all doubtful cases by putting an apostrophe in. This is over-insurance, and produces results like this:

Some student's alway's solve their problem by putting in apostrophe's at all possible place's.

In that example, not one of the apostrophes is correct: most of them are intrusions into ordinary plurals – of the kind we often see on market stalls, as in *Potatoe's 5p** or *Tom's 35p.** Part of the confusion arises from uncertainty about abbreviations in the plural, as in *LEAs, Three MAs and two PhDs* and similar cases, where the apostrophe is often used to mark missing letters but strictly speaking should not be. (LEA's means 'of the one LEA').

The best standard work of reference on all matters of punctuation is Collins—*Authors and Printers Dictionary* (Oxford U.P.).

7
The assignment approach

7.1 Language in real life

7.1.1

Suppose you work as a sales assistant in a shoe shop, and a customer returns a pair of shoes claiming that they are faulty. What should you do or say? You cannot answer this question without knowing something about the firm, your position in it, the customer, the shoes themselves, and the shop's policy in these matters. The use of language you would make in this situation thus depends on your knowledge of the full detail of the situation, and this is true of all use of language in business or administration. In order to provide this kind of detail, for each of our assignments, we have set up a description. The description which introduces each group of assignments we shall call a 'Setting'.

7.1.2

So far, in using this book, you have been concerned with exercises about particular details of language. The purpose of learning these details is to be able to use language efficiently. But there is no point in learning 'good English' just for the sake of it: the point is to be able to use your language to communicate, and that always happens in concrete situations dealing with particular problems.

7.1.3

The basis of the assignments which make up the rest of this book is a set of situations which give rise to a series of communication tasks. We have tried to make these settings and tasks as realistic as possible: all of them are based on events which have actually occurred at some time or another. All of them involve people working together, so that the human relationships aspect is just as important as the communications aspect.

7.1.4

The situations described in our settings are based on fact, but names and places have been changed. Any resemblance to real people or places is quite unintentional.

7.1.5

This approach could well mean a change from the kind of work you have been used to in English. With an assignment approach, there may well not be any 'right' answers: most of the tasks which follow can be carried out in a variety of ways. What matters is to make the answer that you provide fit the needs of the situation. This means that it may not be enough to ensure that a letter is correctly laid out and perfect in punctuation and spelling, although these qualities are certainly necessary. It also needs to have the right tone.

7.1.6

'Tone' refers to the feeling and attitudes which come through from the writer to the reader, and the responses aroused in the reader himself. In section 7.3 we give a set of examples which show several ways of dealing with particular tasks. We shall leave the differences between these examples for you and your teacher to discuss.

7.1.7

Each group of four or five assignments is provided with a setting, followed by a first assignment in which the tasks are concerned with your understanding of the setting itself. This activity of 'comprehension' is important because the tasks in the later assignments cannot be carried out satisfactorily (or, in some cases, at all) if the text of the setting has not been fully understood. You will find repeatedly that the later assignments require you to go back and read the basic setting again.

7.2 The Assignments

7.2.1

The assignments are intended to provide a bank of material for the teacher to draw on according to the needs of the class. It is not intended or possible that a class should work through every assignment. Classes taking a BEC General Level Course will be subject to a set of learning objectives of the Course, and the teacher will select assignments to help the class meet them. Other classes may well pursue quite different sets of assignments.

7.2.2

There are six groups of assignments, each one self-contained. For each group, we have set out to provide in the setting all the information the student will need for the assignments in that group, except where we propose tasks involving a search for information. Within each group, too, each assignment is independent of the others.

7.2.3

The assignments vary in nature and scale. The work to be done may be oral or written, and will include several types of business communication. Many of the tasks are oral because a high proportion of contact in real business life is oral, and the emphasis on discussion is quite deliberate: taking part in discussion, without dominating people on the one hand or being the ever-silent mouse on the other, is something which has to be learned. The amount of time that an assignment will take is also impossible to predict, because different classes will be at different stages in the Course. We know from college trials of the assignments that students who are new to them take much longer over an assignment than those who have experience with the approach. However, no student will need to guess at essential information, since this is provided in every assignment setting, and students who have no experience of business should not be placed at a disadvantage.

7.3 Worked examples

One of the most valuable parts of learning how to write in a business context lies in the close comparison of different versions of the same task. In this section we provide four versions of each of three different tasks, but it should not be assumed that any one of them is automatically a best version.

7.3.1 First example

Suppose you are the assistant to the Manager of a large open-plan office occupied by a typing pool and a group of some twenty finance clerks dealing with wages, orders, payments, etc., in a local authority office. Flexitime is in operation, there are generous tea breaks, but there is a rigid rule against beverages or food being taken to individual desks. The rule is being disregarded, by some section heads as well as juniors.

Task

Your superior asks you to draft a note for distribution to every member of staff with his weekly or monthly payslip, reminding him of the rule. Draft the circular note for the Manager's signature.

Version 1

```
All staff know the rule which forbids
the consumption of food or beverages
of any kind at their desks.  Please
observe it.
```

Version 2

```
I am sorry to have to draw your
attention to the rule forbiding food
or drinks at your desks.  It is being
disregarded by a significant number
of staff, and I have no choice but to
warn that further disregard of it will
oblige me to take disciplinary action.
```

Version 3

```
Ladies and Gentlemen, you all know
quite well that we are not allowed to
bring food or drinks to our desks.  If
the rule is being broken so frequently
that even I can see it every time I
walk through the office, you give me
no choice but to enforce it.  I would
rather not be embarrassed in this way,
but if I do have to come down on it
you will find the process much more
embarrassing still.
```

Version 4

```
"Members of the clerical and adminis-
trative staff in this authority are
prohibited from taking all kinds of
food or beverages to their desks or
workplaces."
(County Code of Practice, 1974, para.
14.7.)
Need I say more!
```

7.3.2 Second example

This example is based on the setting described in chapter 2. After Helen Fowles has moved into her house, and the four other students have joined her, the Gas Board delivers the gas fires which she had bought for the bedrooms. The salesman assured Helen that they would be fitted (i.e. connected to the gas supply) a few days after delivery. The diary reads thus:

```
   August 16th     purchase of gas fires;
                   payment by cheque
September 18th     notification that
                   delivery is required.
September 22nd     delivery of gas fires
September 25th     telephone enquiry ask-
                   ing when fitting would
                   happen:  promise to
                   ring back; no further
                   action.
September 29th     second telephone en-
                   quiry passed from one
                   officer to another;
                   promise to ring back;
                   no further action.
```

October 4th third telephone enquiry; treated much as the second call, with final response 'we can't fit any more fires for the time being – it will be at least three months.'

Task

Write the letter which Helen Fowles has to send complaining about this treatment.

Version 1

General Manager,
Ledsham Area,
South Midland Gas Board.

Dear Sir,

I want to complain about your treatment of me. I bought four gas fires from your Eastern Ledsham office last month and got a guarantee of immediate fitting. They came ten days ago and have still not been fitted. Your woman on the phone today was rude.

                Yours sincerely,

Version 2

Sales Manager,
East Ledsham Showroom,
South Midlands Gas Board.

Dear Sir,

On August 16th last I bought four Goblin gas fires at your showroom, and your salesman promised immediate fitting. They were delivered on September 22nd as I asked but have not been fitted in spite of three telephone calls to your office. Two were ignored and the third time I was told fitting would take three months. Please carry out the fitting as soon as possible or I shall have to take further action.

                Yours faithfully,

Version 3

General Manager,
South Midlands Gas,
Ledsham.

Sir,

On August 16th I bought four Goblin gas fires at your East Ledsham showroom and arranged for delivery to be made on request. I was assured that fitting the fires would be done within a week of delivery. In fact, they were delivered on September 22nd, but have not been fitted yet. I rang the showroom three times, and after a lot of shunting about I was told that I would have to wait at least three months. This isn't good enough: please keep your salesman's promises.

                Yours faithfully,

Version 4

For the personal attention of the Area General Manager, South Midlands Gas.

Dear Sir,

I am sorry to have to trouble you with a problem and would be grateful for your help.

On August 16th I bought four Goblin gas fires at your East Ledsham showroom under the terms of the special offer being made at the time. Your salesman, Mr. Harrison, treated me most courteously, and gave a firm undertaking that fitting would be arranged within a few days of delivery. I paid for the fires by cheque and subsequently arranged delivery which took place on September 22nd. Your invoice number is EL282/119.

Your delivery man suggested that I should telephone the showroom to arrange for fitting. The showroom referred me to Area Service. My call was there passed from one officer to another until a most discourteous lady said that no fitting would be possible for three months.

I have to mention that I am responsible for the welfare of four other students who share this house with me. In advertising your fires, but failing to provide fitting at the start of the heating season, you provide me with a very strong argument. I am sure you would not wish me to make use of this until you have had opportunity to put the situation right.

                Yours faithfully,

7.3.3 Third example

The firm of Ramsey and Foxdale Ltd, (see the fuller account in 4.2) employs a large number of young men and women who come to work on their motor cycles. Thefts of parts, damage to cycles and even thefts of whole machines have become an increasing problem. After some discussion among a number of colleagues, you have put forward the suggestion on their behalf that the employees who use the park contribute to the cost of supervision employed by the firm. In studying the following replies, consider the bearing on the text of who is writing, his rank and status, as well as the way it is worded.

Version 1

MEMORANDUM From: Premises Superintendent
             To: W. L. Gower, Wages Department.
             Subject: Supervision of motorcycle park

Your suggestion for the paid supervision of the m/c park, to be re-charged to using employees, is passed to me for reply. I regret it is impossible for the company to entertain this proposal owing to the legal complications involved.

Version 2

MEMORANDUM From: Personnel Manager
             To: Wages Manager
             copy: W. L. Gower, Wages Dept.

You passed Gower's useful suggestion about supervision of the car park to protect staff motorcycles to me. It is a sensible idea but have Gower and his friends thought about the realities? Would any of them like to be paid for keeping off the thieves and thugs?

Version 3

MEMORANDUM From: Company Secretary
             To: Personnel Manager
             copy: W. L. Gower, Wages Dept.
             Subject: Supervision of Motorcycle Park

Thank you for your query about Mr. Gower's suggestion. It is appreciated that many employees experience this problem and the suggestion is recognised as a serious attempt to resolve it. Unfortunately the legal position of the firm would change if it accepted payment from employees to cover the cost involved. At present employees are liable for damage and loss to their own vehicles when parked on company property. Under the proposed arrangement the liability for every such instance would fall on the firm. The alternative would be for the company to provide supervision without asking employees to pay for it.

Version 4

MEMORANDUM From: Personnel Manager
             To: W. L. Gower, Wages Department
             copy: Manager, Wages Dept.

You will remember suggesting on behalf of a number of your colleagues that the firm should provide a warden for the motorcycle park, charging the cost to the users. This is of course a sensible idea and we should very much have liked to carry it out. There are two difficulties about it.

The first is that the number of motorcyclists among our employees goes up and down very unpredictably. The group between whom the cost would have to be shared could go up to 100, but could fall to as few as 30. You may be willing to pay three times the charge envisaged in your letter, but I doubt if all the other motorcyclists would feel the same.

The other problem will seem to you a technicality, but as things are the users of the park are responsible for their own property, and the company is not liable for theft or loss or, much the more serious aspect, personal accident. Unfortunately the law leaves us no option: if we pay an attendant, we can preserve existing liability, but if the employees contribute, they are held in law to be paying for a service, including the service of becoming liable for theft, loss or accident. My colleagues in the Legal Department are adamant that the firm cannot afford that liability.

7.4 Human relations

In your discussion of the foregoing examples, you may be tempted to suppose that business and administration need to use a special kind of English different from any other kind. This is an illusion. Some officials, it is true, have been trained to write in a cold and formal way, but almost all senior staff in business and local government dislike the use of 'officialese'. The point of using the language is to communicate, not to show that you are an official.

7.4.1

Therefore, if you have a choice between being official and writing in a direct and human way, always choose the latter. If your message is going to be unwelcome, say 'we are sorry to have to tell you . . .' rather than 'we regret' or (worse) 'it is regretted that'. Again, if the message is pleasurable, say 'I am glad to tell you' not 'it gives me pleasure to inform you'. Communication is not separate from human relations: the one is part of the other. There are times when to be clear and concise is not enough, and indeed when in order to be courteous and human it might be necessary to write at greater length.

Assignments – Group 1
Millar's Motors

Manderby is a medium-sized industrial town in central England which developed strongly in the middle of the last century as a centre of metal industries. Hubert Millar set up in business there in 1878 as a coach builder. With the coming of the motor car the firm became one of the town's motor agencies. It had its ups and downs over the years, but for most of its history was based firmly on its service side. In the early 1960s the proprietors built a large new service shop on very advanced lines, with five servicing 'tracks', much modern equipment, and a substantial staff led by five foremen and a manager. The sudden death of Sir Humphrey Millar, the last member of the family, in 1968 brought about the sale of the business to a group of businessmen.

The new owners appointed ambitious young managers to run the firm and placed the main emphasis on developing the sales side of the business. The performance of each section of the firm was assessed every month on the basis of figures. Turnover in the sales side and turn-round in the service division became all-important. Managers who let the figures slip were liable to be dismissed, and Alex Smart, the current General Manager, is a product of that hard school. Now 38, he began as a car salesman, became Sales Manager, and won promotion by the performance he gave in his job. Naturally, he views the service side as there to serve the needs of the sales side, and this makes for strained relationships with some of the service personnel.

George Binney, the Servicing Manager, is a skilled engineer with a genius for diagnosing mechanical trouble. He has been with the firm for thirty years and still believes in high standards of workmanship, but his powers of leadership have enabled him to survive in the new regime.

He does not particularly like the incentive schemes which give the servicing teams a bonus based on turnover, and provide the most 'successful' foreman of the year with a new car. The manufacturers of cars provide service manuals which set out recommended times for each servicing operation, and Binney interprets these as the shortest, not the longest times for work. The management, however, insists on the opposite view, and Binney has learnt to keep his dislike to himself.

The Sales Manager, Stuart Ingram, is an ambitious young man, charming to customers, and impatient with Binney's perfectionist views. Fairly soon after his appointment some years ago, Ingram succeeded in persuading the firm to transfer the parts and stores section from the service department to his own. There is a serious debate going on among the management over his demand that one of the service tracks be turned over to Ingram's control for the purpose of running the pre-delivery inspections (or PDIs) on new cars. Ingram is also aiming at having his car hire section transferred from the Accountant's control to his own.

Assignment 1A – Understanding the picture

1. **What do you understand by** the phrase 'diagnosing mechanical trouble', and why should a genius for this particular activity be valuable to a Servicing Manager?
2. **Explore in discussion** the nature of the disagreement between Binney and his superiors over the service times.
3. **Explore** how the firm's staffing before Sir H. Millar's death would have appeared in an organisation chart.
4. **Explore in discussion** how the organisation chart of the firm given below reveals the changes which Ingram has brought about, and redraw the chart to show what Ingram would like it to be.

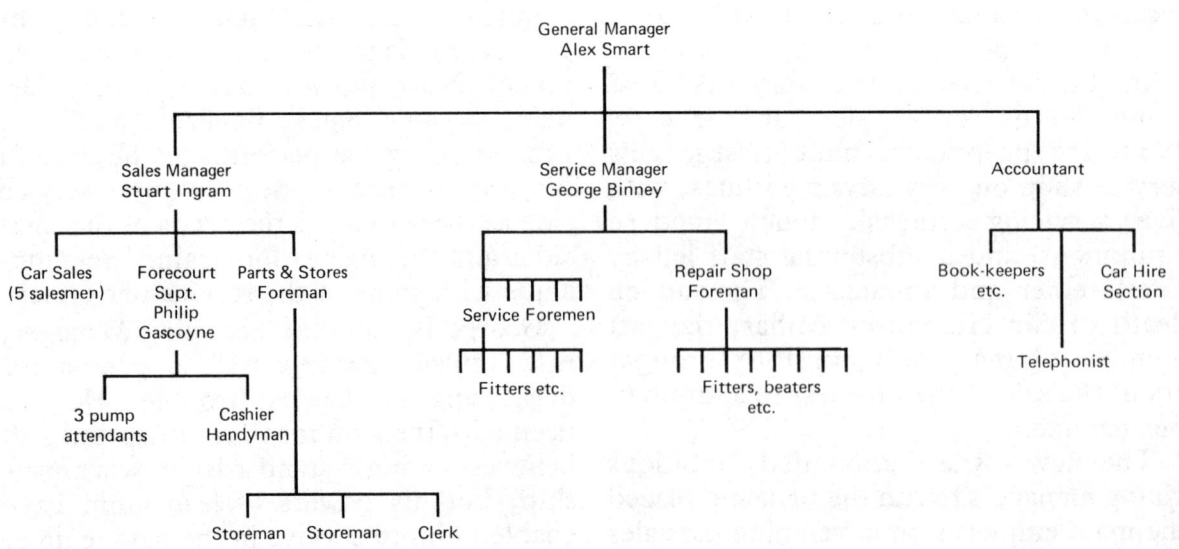

Assignment 1B – Len Forsyth

Len Forsyth is 17½ and has worked at Millar's for fourteen months as a pump attendant. In the early part of the summer he had four half-days of absence owing to asthma which was triggered by hay fever and in September was away for six working days with influenza, sending in the proper medical certificates. A week later he went to collect his pay packet from the Forecourt Superintendent, Philip Gascoyne, who handed it to him saying 'There are two weeks' wages there, Forsyth, you needn't come in again – we've had more than enough of your absences.' It was the first hint of criticism that Forsyth had had, apart from a passing joke from one of the other pump attendants in June. Len suspects that he is being made the victim of declining sales in petrol and asks to see the Sales Manager. Gascoyne replies, 'No good, Forsyth! This was the boss's decision, and he's away on business until Wednesday. You'd better put it in writing. Now we don't want to see you on the premises again.' Len goes away, wondering what he can do, if anything, about his dismissal.

Task 1

Find out your rights under the Employment Protection Act. Your teacher may give you a prepared oral briefing, or ask you to investigate. Make rough notes on your information, without attempting to write down in full everything you are told. **Write up the rough notes for your file.**

Task 2

On the basis of your notes **write a letter to Mr Smart** suggesting that you have been unfairly dismissed. Do not make any threats, ask for the matter to be reconsidered, and request an interview.

Task 3

After some days Smart sends for you, and offers you an alternative job as Assistant in the Spares and Stores. Your previous job was paid on a weekly basis for a 42-hour week, but this one is hourly-paid for a 37-hour week and will bring in less money. However, it is indoor work which should help the asthma, so you decide to accept it. But Smart then tells you that you cannot begin work for four more weeks, leaving you unemployed and unpaid for two weeks. **Discuss Len's dilemma:** should he accept the job and allow the firm to get away with an unfair dismissal, or refuse the offer and claim compensation, knowing that the firm can say it has offered him alternative work?

Task 4

Len decides, rightly or wrongly, to accept the situation, but he is advised to insist on having a contract of employment. **Work out in discussion** a list of points which the contract ought to include.

Assignment 1C – Episodes on the forecourt

In the event, Len was not out of work in the intervening two weeks: he was brought back as a forecourt attendant to cover the 'after hours' work between 1700 and 1930 when the forecourt for petrol sales was the only part remaining open. One of the senior sales staff is usually on the premises for this period, but the following episodes occur while the salesman of the day is out demonstrating a car to a customer who has made an appointment.

Task 1

A respectably dressed man in a very expensive car drives up and is served with 7 gallons of petrol. He searches his pockets and then declares that he has left his wallet in the office and does not carry cash. **Discuss how Len should respond to this situation.**

Task 2

Ingram briefs Len before going home one evening about a secondhand Cortina: 'A Mr Hudson will be bringing in his old car at 7 o'clock with a cheque for £300. You know the rule – no cheque, no keys.' When Hudson arrives he hands over a cheque but it is for £150, and he says he will bring in the rest the next day. **Discuss the encounter or write and act a play version of it in which Ingram's instructions are carried out.**

Task 3

At 18.15 the Parts and Spares Foreman, who will be Len's boss from the following Monday, helps himself to 4 gallons of petrol, gets into his car and calls out, 'You know how to fix the books, don't you, Len.' What would you do if you were Len?

Task 4

A young man drives up in a car which you suspect to be stolen: he is very shabbily dressed to be driving so expensive a vehicle. He tries to help himself to some of the goods in the forecourt shop and when you try to stop him, threatens you with a razor. Thinking of a person known to you, preferably a volunteer member of the class, **write a description of the thief** which would enable the police to identify him.

Assignment 1D—New recruit

Two years have passed and Len Forsyth has made an outstanding success of his job as Parts Storeman. The first Foreman has left the department, and the new one, George Briggs, is only three years older than Len himself. The other Storeman also left recently, and Ingram does not want to be bothered with the chores of appointing the replacement. He has laid down that the job should be advertised rather than filled through the agencies or careers service, and while he refuses to have a completely raw school leaver, the rate for the job is unlikely to attract many applicants. The job is not totally straight-forward: the parts catalogue of the company concerned is now held on microfiche, so that each page has to be projected on a screen, and the lighting makes the screen difficult to read. Each part has a code number, running to nine letters and digits, which has to be read with great care. The clerical work involved is detailed, but at the same time many of the parts are oily and the accountant's department insists that the paper be clean. Ideally, the job calls for some knowledge of cars and how they work, and for some skill in dealing with customers.

Task 1

Draft any advertisements you would use in recruiting such a person.

Task 2

As one of the applicants for the job, **draft a letter** asking your former head teacher to serve as a referee for the application.

Task 3

Just over two weeks later the manager tells the Stores Foreman (Briggs) that he has had a score of applications, but is taking only five of them seriously. He has talked to a previous employer in each case and wants a written confidential reference from each one's previous school. **Draft a letter** asking one of the head teachers for such a reference, for Mr Ingram to sign.

Task 4

Ingram has handed Briggs the details of the candidates for the post but does not pass on the references or the applications. He tells Briggs to interview the candidates and to bring in the selected one for him to see. Briggs asks you to take part in the interviewing and warns you to be ready with some good questions. Working in groups, **devise a set of questions** and **make a set of notes** of the items which the interview should cover. If time allows, **set up a simulation** of the interviews.

CANDIDATES FOR POST OF STOREMAN, MILLAR'S MOTORS LTD.

Name	Age	School	Qualifications	Job Experience	Interests	Other information
Michael McGuire Flat 5, 68 Avon St Manderby	17.4	Burnside Compr.	CSE 5 Subj.	Work expce scheme (Hotel kitchen)	pop music	has driving lic.
Judith Cairns 5 Horton Road Hallingtree	17.8	St. Cecilia's R.C. Compr.	4 O Levels. on BEC course	Father's farm office	archaeology horses	used to farm machinery drives tractor, can type. Just married (runaway?)
Mark Dodgson 18 Crossgreen Place Manderby	16.9	Burnside Compr.	CSE 3 subjs.	nil	m/cycles (owns 2) scrambling	Worked newsagent shop wk-ends since age 14.
Tariq Mohammed c/o Ali 116c Grey Street Manderby	17.9	Falkland Compr.	3 CSE's 2 O Levels on BEC course	labourer with local builder	sport	sch prefect, socc. capt. swimming capt. driving licence.
Wesley Monroe 19 Howard Street Manderby	17.3	Falkland Compr.	2 O Levels	Storeman, local hardware shop.	sport	Member of England U18 Basketball team.

Assignments – Group 2
Hunter Coaches Ltd

Ernest Holbrook and his brother Bernard learned to drive as soldiers in World War I, and in 1920 set up business with a couple of Army surplus lorries. Working in Central and Northern Manchester they carried any commodity they could find. They fitted the lorries with removable wooden seats and tarpaulin covers for transporting people, but there were many competitors in the area and the brothers only scraped a living. Very gradually the passenger-carrying business became more important, and in 1925 they were able to acquire a real bus.

From the early 1930s the business prospered. During the Second World War it ran fifty commuter journeys every day to armaments factories in the area, and the period of petrol rationing after the war saw a minor boom in coach touring. The rapid spread of car ownership in the period between 1950 and 1965 brought a sharp reduction in commuter contract business, and the Holbrooks turned instead to developing holiday tours. In conjunction with a handful of specialist agencies overseas, the firm began to use carefully chosen and highly paid couriers and guides to lead specialist tours which travelled on the best coaches money could buy. The coming of the breathalyser also created a lucrative business in the hire of minibuses.

In 1973 the firm became a private limited company and was put in the charge of Ernest's son, Charles. Since then it had become superbly organised, able to mount tours at several different levels of the market, and in a unique position for overseas tourists: no other coach firm outside London could offer a skilled guide in any major language of the world.

The fleet now consists of three Fiat air-conditioned steel-framed 50-seater coaches, a similar coach of 24 seats, a score of single decker British made saloon coaches of varying sizes, two dozen double deckers bought second-hand from urban Transport Undertakings, and four mini-buses respectively seating 10, 12, 18 and 20. The elderly double deckers are used for commuter services to suburban factories, but the rest of the fleet is kept in prime condition, and no vehicle is more than four years old. The firm has always refused to carry supplies of alcoholic drink on its coaches, and keeps a strict limit on its commitments to football supporters and school outings.

The emphasis on catering for overseas tourists in their own languages arises from Ernest Holbrook's wife, Maria. She grew up in Austria speaking three languages herself, and first met her husband when she worked for the firm as a guide. She still works in the business, mainly on contacting travel agencies overseas and on the planning of the firm's two annual tours on the continent.

Assignment 2A – Understanding the picture

1. **Explain** the connection between having many competitors and being able only to 'scrape a living'.
2. The second paragraph lists three developments in the history of the firm and suggests a cause for each. In the case of the first, **explain** why coach touring should boom in a time of petrol rationing. **Identify** the other two developments which are given suggested causes, and show in each case how cause and effect are related.
3. What is a private limited company, and how it is different from a public one? Why should it be better for this firm to be a private company?
4. What languages come under the heading of the 'major languages of the world'?

Assignment 2B – Coach bookings

You work in the general office of Hunter Coaches Ltd as a Reservations Clerk, and deal with most of the routine booking requests for ordinary coaches. There is a standard treatment for each request. If the reservation board shows that a suitable vehicle is free, a blue tag is inserted for the date. The tag bears a number, which is in turn used for coding the request, and a positive reply is sent enclosing a form asking for details of the journey, the numbers and other information which the firm must have if it is to run its business efficiently. The booking is provisional until this form is received, but when it comes in the blue tag is replaced with a green one, a confirmation is sent, and a further confirmation is sent out ten days before the date of the reservation. For new clients, and for journeys longer than a single day, a deposit is always required.

Task 1

Design the form described above.

Task 2

Draft a letter in reply to the following request:

                                                        19 Rugby Avenue,
                                                        Terrington,
                                                        Macclesfield,
                                                        Cheshire.

Drivers Hire Department,   2nd August.
Hunters Coaches Ltd.,
Macadam Road,
MANCHESTER.

Dear Sirs,

    I wish to arrange for a party to travel from Macclesfield to Doncaster for the St. Leger Race Meeting on September 14th. We require a 40-seater coach for the day and would like the driver to be Maurice Bedford, who took us to the Leger last year.

    Please send me a quotation so that I can make arrangements for the rest of the party.

                                                        Yours faithfully,

Task 3

The secretary of a local Rugby club telephones and asks if a coach is available to take two teams and a small group of supporters to a fixture at Abergele three weeks on Saturday. The club in question has a well-deserved reputation for heavy drinking on the return journey. **Simulate the telephone conversation** with the applicant, who is very persistent.

Task 4

A local Canoe Club seeks a booking to take 26 of its members to Derwentwater, and asks by telephone for a double decker so that 14 of its GRP one-seater kayaks can go too. This request has previously been met by using one of the commuter traffic double deckers, but most of these are now in very poor condition inside, though perfectly roadworthy. **Draft a reply** to the request, worded in such a way that the Canoe Club is not put off, but has no basis for complaint afterwards if it finds the bus of rather poor quality.

Assignment 2C – Valley Forge Tours

In several big cities in the USA there exist specialised small travel agencies which grew up by catering for parties of Americans who wanted to go 'ancestor hunting' in the United Kingdom. For example, an agent would recognise strong family connections with say, South Devon, would visit the area to make arrangements, and organise a coach tour. A group of about 20 would visit the area where their families originated, have lectures by specialists in family history, study parish records, and so on. This type of business was later developed into tours catering for other special-interest groups — a typical year in the mid-70's saw groups visiting country houses, rose gardens, private libraries, industrial archaeology, and private art collections. Because they are small and expensive, such tours can often visit houses which are not open to the general public.

One of these agencies is in Philadelphia and is run by a Miss Elaine Manaheim. Her particular interest is country houses, and she spends much of the winter in England organising the tours. She runs parties limited to 22 members, and has a long-term contract with Hunter Coaches, on the strength of which the firm bought a special coach from an Italian supplier, fitted with air conditioning and every modern luxury. Miss Manaheim's firm, Valley Forge Tours, advertises that every tour is personally guided by herself, with a driver who knows the country and a nurse-courier to look after the participants.

Miss Manaheim makes all the arrangements for visits and accommodation of the tour party and herself. She expects Hunter Coaches to provide the coach, the driver, the nurse and their accommodation. Her season offers thirteen tours lasting 13 or 14 days each, with two 3-day breaks between tours, and extends from mid-April to early October. The firm uses two drivers doing alternate tours but one nurse-courier.

Task 1

During the winter Miss Manaheim writes to ask whether the following itinerary can be managed on a 13-day or 14-day tour without breaking her rule of keeping any one day's travel to less than 100 miles:
Heathrow – Hungerford – Salisbury – Mere (Wilts) – Yeovil – Exeter – Ilfracombe – Dorchester – Lyme Regis – Weymouth – Chichester – Arundel – Winchester – Windsor.

Work out the answer to her question, and **suggest changes** in the route which might reduce the distance travelled.

Task 2

The tour just studied is in fact fairly typical: They travel up to 80 miles a day at most and often only 30 miles. On that basis you can work out the normal touring season mileage for the coach. On the basis of the current price of diesel fuel, **what is the firm's fuel bill** for the Valley Forge tours programme?

Task 3

During the winter it is necessary to advertise for a nurse-courier. The job lasts for only six months with very little time off and calls for unusual qualities: many of the tourists are elderly and, being wealthy, are used to having servants. The rate of pay is enough to provide the equivalent, in the six months, of a year's income for a private nurse. Hunters decide to fill the post through a commercial agency, which asks for

1. a job-description in less than 50 words for their short-notices list
2. a job-description giving as much information as possible within a typescript of one side of headed A4 paper.

Draft these two documents.

Task 4

Hunters have to arrange accommodation for the nurse and the driver for every overnight stop throughout the touring season. **Draw up the text** of a standard booking-letter in which places, dates, and any other relevant details can be filled in for making reservations.

Assignment 2D – Managing the office

The Manager of the general office at Hunter Coaches is Bernie Denis, who was one of the firm's drivers before the war. He came back from the Navy determined to 'better himself', and worked steadily through night school to gain a string of City and Guilds Certificates. He is proud of having 'come up the hard way', and is therefore not very fond of day-release. You have worked in the department for three years since leaving school, and are one of the more experienced and established clerks in the office. The firm supports the Road Transport Industry Training Board and encourages its staff to seek further qualifications. You took the firm up on this for your BEC General Level course and hope to go on to National Level. Although the firm's support in principle is clear, the decision in any particular case rests with the section head. When you approach Mr Denis with a request for day release for two years to take National Level he asks you to put it in writing. You sense that this is really a way of putting you off.

Task 1

Discuss in class the arguments to use, including those which it would be wiser to avoid using in this particular case.

Task 2

Write a suitable memorandum to Mr Denis explaining what you hope to gain from a BEC National Course and what you think the firm might gain from it also.

Task 3

Denis responds to your memo by calling you in and giving you a job to do. He says, 'The boss and I have been watching the lists of requests on our Answerphone Service tapes. It's clear that people don't know how to handle an Answerphone, and we are losing a good deal of business by shutting down the enquiry office when we do. We really need to arrange to man the enquiry counter and phone every lunch hour, for an hour after normal closing each day, from one till six on Saturdays and eleven till four on Sundays. I want two people on together on Sundays. We shall be paying overtime at time-and-a-half and double time for Sunday work, but I don't want anyone doing more than one Sunday in three. **Would you sort out a rota that will work**, and I will go through it with you.'

The normal hours of work for the firm are 0900 to 1200 and 1330 to 1700, with 0900–1300 Saturdays. The personnel concerned are as follows:

1. Sandra Mulligan – $2\frac{1}{2}$ years' service as shorthand typist; only recently moved into Reservations Clerk work.
2. Ellen Wilkinson – $16\frac{1}{2}$, recently appointed; good at filing, interested in timetables, has an unfortunate manner with women enquirers.
3. Dora Totley – has been Reservations Clerk for almost two years, a good friend of yours. Refuses to work with Sandra Mulligan.
4. Tony Grey – a driver with the firm for ten years, recently taken off driving because of suspected epilepsy. 'Filling in' with office work, which he does well but finds frustrating.

5. Diane Butler – very patient with vague or muddled enquirers; a former university student who keeps the fact quiet, she has worked during vacations as a minibus driver and a coach tour guide.

6. Nirmal Singh Gupta – a recent school leaver with perfect English and a number of good O-Level results. Very co-operative.

Task 4

You anticipate that the rota will not be difficult to organise or carry out, but that Saturday afternoon sessions will be distinctly unpopular. **Simulate the conversation** in which you offer to Bernie Denis to undertake two of these afternoon sessions out of three if he will grant you day release. He complains bitterly that you ought to do the course by night school as he did, and cannot understand that the course is simply not available as a night school option: it only exists as a course using a full day and an additional evening. He is also unaware of the fact that the course is much more demanding than most of those which he undertook as a student.

Assignments Group 3
Riddles Limited

Riddles and Company was a family-run lock-up hardware store which merged during the war with its neighbour, a household draper. A few years later the combined shop was taken over by a sports goods dealer as part of a national chain. This chain consists of a number of similar stores, all based on the same pattern of merging two or three neighbouring businesses in the centre of medium-sized towns. The chain likes to preserve much of the local character of its stores, and the three joined-up shops now known as Riddles Limited form a medium-sized department store.

The original hardware shop now forms the departments which sell cutlery, kitchen hardware, china and glass and related items. The cutlery department, however, is unique, selling a huge range of single items and all kinds of sets of table cutlery short of solid silver. There is much stainless steel tableware on display and the department has a reputation for providing specialist cutlery all over the North of England.

Most of the staff are young women shop assistants, and staff turnover is fairly high. Nevertheless, the business is well run and adequately profitable. The more experienced and senior sales staff receive good bonuses, customers are loyal, and the shop has an air of well-mannered calm. The cutlery department is run by a senior sales assistant, Mary Kenyon, and two young women assistants. It comes under the hardware buyer, Jonas Greenyer, who is responsible in turn to the Deputy Manager, Harold Bayliss, and the General Manager, James Riddles. Bayliss deals with personnel and staff matters, customers' complaints, and the despatch and delivery side. He is aged 61 and gentle in manner but very tough underneath. Riddles, a very distant relative of the founder, is a university graduate with a flair for display, a specialised training in retail management and a very good head for figures.

The shop is arranged traditionally, with sales counters on each side of a corridor-pattern layout, and a cash desk for every pair of counters. Riddles has recently converted the stock control to a computer storage system which is 'fed' from each electronic till. This provides him with very close checks on stocks and sales, and it is rumoured among the staff that a blitz against shop-lifting and pilfering is immediately impending. Certainly, the notices that shop-lifters would always be prosecuted in the courts have recently been renewed.

Assignment 3A – Understanding the picture

1. What can you work out from the description given above about the amount of space in the shops originally occupying the building and the space in the current department store? On the assumption that there are five main departments in each store in the chain, some of them divided into sections, what changes would you expect to have taken place to convert three separate lock-up shops into such a department store?

2. The Manager, James Riddles, is described as having a specialist training for retail management and three other attributes. In what ways might these attributes help to make him a good retail manager, and what other particular attributes would he need?

3. By reference to the layout of particular shops which you know, explore in discussion the relationship between some types of layout in shops and the frequency of shoplifting. For example, is it true that some stores are laid out in a way which encourages it?

4. Obtain information on computerised systems of stock- and cash-control which are becoming common in retailing and explore their effects on junior sales staff.

Assignment 3B – Mrs Shaw's weakness

You are Janice Belling and aged 19. You have worked as a shop assistant at Riddles ever since leaving school. After six months working in several departments, you have worked happily under Mrs Kenyon in cutlery and have come to know the stock very well. Indeed, you and she now possess a highly-developed 'nose' for what is in stock, and believe that the new computer-based stock control system will teach you little you do not already know about your section.

The store as a whole has a number of middle-aged women customers who come in quite regularly, more often to look than to buy, but when they do make a purchase it is usually substantial. One of these is Mrs Shaw, a neighbour of your uncle who lives in a distinctly upper-crust part of town. One day when she wanders through the department inspecting the displays you are busy serving and scarcely notice her, but out of the corner of your eye catch a movement which makes you suspicious. Next time she comes in you watch more carefully, and become almost certain that she is engaged in some modest but skilful shop-lifting. The contrast between her respectable appearance and her deft way with the goods is hard to believe, and you doubt whether your superiors would believe it either.

On a third occasion you see Mrs Shaw, and watch her closely. You now become quite convinced that she has stolen a small but expensive stainless steel dish.

Task 1

Discuss in class the alternatives which are open to you at this stage. Consider especially whether you should report the matter formally, or whether, since you and Mrs Shaw know each other by name (although she has not recognised you), it would be better to warn her privately that she is being spotted.

Task 2

You decide to ask Mrs Kenyon to keep an eye out for Mrs Shaw herself. When Mrs Shaw next appears, Mrs Kenyon is in the stockroom. Mrs Shaw goes straight through to the kitchenware, a department which you can see clearly from your own counter, and there, to your astonishment, she slips five items in quick succession into her bag. This time another assistant has seen her and calls Mr Bayliss, who stops her as she leaves the store and asks her to accompany him to this office. After protests, she agrees and the facts are revealed. **Find out the exact legal position** of the Deputy Manager in these circumstances. (Does he have any right to detain or search? What could he have done if Mrs Shaw had refused to co-operate?)

Task 3

Write a note of instruction to young sales assistants about how to deal with cases of suspected shop-lifting.

Task 4

Mrs Shaw admits the five thefts in the bag and claims that she has never taken anything before. It is a once-for-all oddity: after all, she says, she is not poor. Mr Bayliss adheres to the firm's rules, sends for a Police Officer, and Mrs Shaw is duly charged. **Discuss in class whether you should reveal** that you know that Mrs Shaw has stolen before. You saw her taking the five items, and are therefore a material witness. You may well be asked, therefore, why you were watching, and, if you had suspicions, why you had not reported them.

Task 5

Mr Riddles demands a written report on the matter from each member of the staff involved. **Write Janice Belling's report** in the form of a memorandum which should be as concise as possible.

Assignment 3C – The bus strike

One autumn, Mr Bayliss offers you a new post in the firm as Clerical Officer in the staffing section, virtually as one of his two immediate assistants, at a considerably higher salary. When you have settled into the work, a dispute over holiday pay arises in the local transport system and develops to the point where a bus strike is likely. This could be very serious for Riddles because most of the firm's staff depend on the buses to get to work.

Mr Bayliss goes through the staff, and arranges for those who travel to work by car and have parking places to give lifts to as many colleagues as possible. This leaves 29 employees, most of whom live in the outer suburbs of the town, who would not have transport. He organises a coach from Fleet Hire Coaches Ltd of Marlborough Street, and asks you to arrange the route and timings for six pick-up points in the morning and six set-down points in the evening.

Task 1

Study the map of the town on p. 99. Mr Bayliss gives you a list of stopping points as follows:

1. The main entrance of the Lemeford General Hospital in Northumberland Road.
2. Outside the Holmeside Comprehensive School in Willand Road.
3. St Peter's Church in College Road.
4. Harma Way south of the Manningtree Road island.
5. The King George IV Bridge at the main GPO building in Queensway.

Plan a route for the coach which will start at the Fleet Hire Depot and end at Riddles and Company timed to bring the staff to work at not later than 0840, with evening departure at 1750.

Task 2

Put this information into a circular letter to staff including a tear-off slip indicating where each member of staff would wish to be picked up and set down.

Task 3

Your replacement in the cutlery section was Cathy Broomfield, who will want to come to work on the bus and lives in Oudenarde Street near the school. It is a Friday, and the strike is due to start the following day. You telephone Cathy's home and discover that she will not be back until Sunday night. Her mother is partially sighted and cannot write anything down. **Make notes for a message which Mrs Broomfield can remember clearly enough** to ensure that Cathy gets the information she needs.

Task 4

The beginning of the strike leads the Traffic Division of the local Police Force to ask the major employers in the town for details of their arrangements to bring staff to work. When you read your circular letter over the telephone to the Traffic Division on the Tuesday afternoon, the officer points out that most of your stopping places are at points which will already be subject to heavy congestion for traffic. He refers to vehicles bringing patients and staff to the Hospital, or staff and pupils to the School. He instructs that the stopping points be moved to be at least a hundred yards clear of each such point of congestion. You now have to revise your route and stopping places accordingly, and **prepare a circular for issue to all members of staff travelling on the bus.**

Assignment 3D – Office routines and problems

Task 1

The new system of stock control works by recording all sales by electronic pulses from each till. An electronic scanner is used to take stock of what is on display, in the stockroom, and so on. Each section can therefore receive a sales and 'losses' figure every day, although in fact Mr Riddles has settled on issuing this once a week. He is quite properly concerned about losses, which can only be due to theft, pilfering or staff errors, but cannot penalise staff for them. He decides instead to offer a pay bonus to the staff of those sections which show no losses or the lowest loss rate among the departments each week. You and Mrs Kenyon have had a knowledge of your stock which has meant that your losses figure has been the best in the store for over two years, and this has never been recognised. You and she are therefore somewhat annoyed, and feel that a memorandum should be written to Mr Riddles informing him of your view. **Write the text of the memorandum** which makes positive suggestions.

Task 2

The company's conditions of service state that the staff's hours of work start twenty minutes before the opening time and end twenty minutes after the closing time in the store. These periods of twenty minutes are known as 'Tidy Time', and are an accepted part of the routine. However, one of the packers in Despatch is a keen union man, and sets out to recruit members. He claims that if more than half the staff joined the union and the union is recognised for negotiating purposes, it would be able to have the 'Tidy Time' recognised as overtime and paid at time-and-a-half. About tolerating the union in general the management of the chain is neutral, and genuinely believes that the wishes of each store's staff should prevail. **List the arguments** for and against the packer's case.

Task 3

The sales staff are on a rota to ensure that they do not work more than two consecutive Saturdays and have a weekly afternoon off. Other part-time staff come in to cover for Saturdays and other times as necessary. Your own new job gives you every Saturday and one afternoon a week free, except at the time of the January and July sales. One of the part-timers is a cousin of yours, married to a professional golfer who wants her to go with him for a tournament overseas. This would mean missing a Wednesday afternoon and a Saturday, and she asks you to 'cover' for her. You do not expect Mr Bayliss to like this request, but you have a strong sense of obligation to your cousin who has done much to help you in the past. Such requests have to go to Mr Bayliss in writing. **Draft the memorandum required.**

Task 4

Collections for presents to members of staff have become very frequent: in the course of a single week you have been asked to support them for the engagement of a clerk you have never met, the retirement of a section head you scarcely know, and the marriages of two saleswomen. Discussion with immediate colleagues led to an informal talk with Mr Bayliss, who suggested that the group of you draw up a set of guidelines to bring the matter under reasonable control. **Draw up the guidelines** for sending to Mr Bayliss.

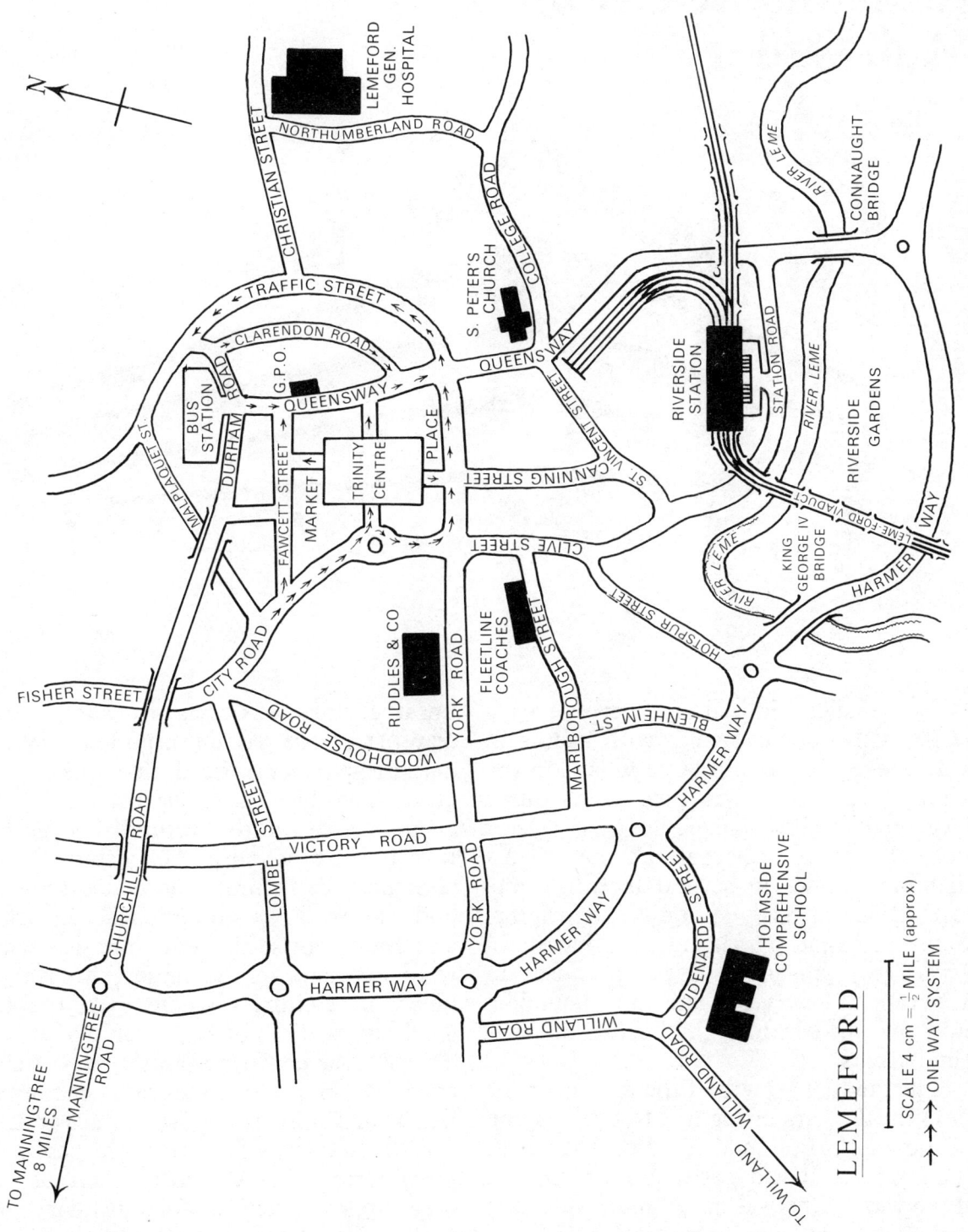

Assignment Group 4
Mail Order

Wilson-Waller Limited of Liverpool are a large mail order company with agents in almost every town and large village in the United Kingdom. The firm sends out a large and weighty catalogue twice a year, but the issue celebrating the firm's diamond jubilee in several months' time is a rather special edition. The original founders began by setting up a bazaar in Ormskirk, moved to larger premises in Liverpool a few years later and launched into mail order through the use of part-time agents.

The gradual growth of the firm over the next thirty years brought it to rank as one of the four largest mail order companies in the country. It had particular strength in three ways. One was an absolute rule that any customer who returned goods as unsatisfactory was always offered refund or replacement without argument. Wilson and his partner argued that even if the goods had been used or broken by the customer, to refuse a refund was the best way of making sure the customer went elsewhere in future. The company's second feature was a strong market in British and European settlements overseas which were not part of the largest British colonies, in countries where even the best local shops did not cater for expatriates. Thirdly, the company built up a particular expertise in packing delicate or complex items for shipment overseas. As a result it was the first large firm to see the packaging possibilities of expanded polystyrene, and it set up a very successful subsidiary company to develop this market.

The basis of the business in the use of part-time agents was very successful for a long time, because its commission was generous and its co-ordination of agents relied on an adequate and well-trained staff of managers. In recent years the company has found it more difficult to recruit suitable part-time agents, and has developed a network of full-time ones. It has just over 400 senior full-time agents to co-ordinate the work of almost 5,000 part-timers, together with a further 900 full-time agents who work independently. The top management is very fond of comparing the total staffing of large retail shop businesses with their turnover figures, in order to show that Wilson-Waller has, per head of its staff, about four times as much turnover as any ordinary shop. Most of the full-time agents work from home, but some have offices which they finance out of their commission income. The really successful full-time agent can earn a good living, but to maintain a high income over a long period is unusual because the market which that calls for is liable to be taken up by retail businesses moving into it. The vast majority of agents earn much less, and a part-time agent does well to earn more than £500 or £600 a year.

Assignment 4A – Understanding the picture

1. Small communities of British people living overseas, in places like Sarawak, Mauritius, or the Pacific islands, were often unable to shop locally. What kinds of goods would they order from such a firm as Wilson-Waller?
2. Why would expanded polystyrene be particularly likely to interest a mail order firm with a large overseas market?
3. What qualities would you expect a firm like this to look for in selecting and appointing (a) part-time and (b) full-time agents?
4. The firm maintains the policy of always replacing or refunding for unsatisfactory goods. This makes it possible for the unscrupulous to exploit the firm, either by ordering goods to use them once and then return them, or by ordering goods with no intention of paying for them. What steps should the firm take to protect itself against each of these possibilities?

Assignment 4B – The Executive Assistant

Anne Taylor is 22 and has worked for Wilson-Waller for over two years. She began as a shorthand-typist at head office, but in due course became secretary to the Agents Manager for the Western Region, who found her alert and willing to take decisions. The Manager offered her the chance to spend two months in the field as a trainee agent, and in the course of her work for him she came across much evidence of the successes and mistakes which agents can make on the job. A great many agents in the region came to rely on her good sense and good advice. The following jobs arise in the course of Anne Taylor's work.

Task 1

An agent in Bristol telephones about her monthly list of delayed and missing payments. These include a sum of £14 owed by a Mrs Mary Williams of 19 Talbot Avenue, Batheaston, and a sum of £7 from Miss Heather Williams of the same address. The agent and Miss Taylor both know the company rule that any one customer's debt is confidential and never revealed to another customer. The part-time agent is competent but does not feel very sure about dealing with this particular situation, and asks Miss Taylor for advice as to how to proceed. If you think that the agent should proceed by writing letters, **draft the necessary text.** If you think the agent should go to call, **arrange a simulation** of a visit to both the ladies who are in debt to the company, who are at home at the same time. (They may be mother and daughter, or wife and sister-in-law.)

Task 2

An agent in Gloucester telephones about a series of orders from a Mr W. L. Gathercole at 17 Homer Drive. The agent concerned has her own office at 42 Cole Court, and points out that the order was incorrectly filled in. In the section of the order form headed 'address for delivery of goods' the customer incorrectly inserted the address of the agent. As a result a nest of tables and a set of garden furniture have already been delivered to the agent's office. The agent points out on the telephone that there is a second order, bearing the same date, for a consignment including a wardrobe and dressing table suite in which the same mistake has been made. She tartly observes that such a consignment could not be got through the door of her own office, let alone accommodated inside it. The order in question bears the number W/LC/79/43875. You telephone the Despatch Manager, and find that he is out: his secretary is engaged and your call is referred to a shorthand-typist. **Dictate a message** which will correct the delivery address mistake as a matter of urgency.

Task 3

Another agent telephones, reporting that her commission account has arrived covering the three months just ended. By some mistake in the machinery, the decimal point between pounds and pence has been shifted one place to the left throughout the account, which gives a balance due to the agent of £191.80. **Write the memorandum** to the accounts office which will get the error corrected, giving the code number of the agent, namely W/RF/289B.

Task 4

The regional agents manager has to organise his share of the company's jubilee celebrations, including regional parties for the senior agents. The manager says this:

'Here is a list of our most experienced part-time agents. There are 55 of them, all women, nearly all well into their 50s. You know they live all over the region. Would you work out the simplest solution to the problem of how to give them a party they will enjoy. It doesn't have to be the cheapest method. You can tell me the where, the when, the what to lay on, the transport, the lot.'

Set out your response in a memorandum.

Assignment 4C – Setting up an office

In the course of the following two years Anne Taylor gains wider experience of agency work, taking charge of an agency in Bristol for six months while the local full-time agent is on maternity leave. Shortly after coming back from Bristol she marries a teacher named Burgess who subsequently gains promotion to a post 15 miles from the new town of Telford in Shropshire. The Western Region Agents Manager realises that there is a job for her to do in Telford: several part-time agents have moved to the new town already, as their husbands or families have gone to live and work there and there is a very active market for the firm's goods. It is just the right time to put in a full-time agent to co-ordinate the part-timers.

Task 1

Discuss in small groups what information Mrs Burgess will need in order to make an intelligent decision in reply to this offer, and what factors she needs to take into account in reaching it.

Task 2

Make a systematic written list of the factors for and against the decision to go to Telford as a full-time agent. Mrs Burgess can reasonably expect to earn £5,000 a year before tax, but she would have to provide her own car, and there would be a moral obligation on her to work for Wilson-Waller for at least two years.

Task 3

Put yourself in the position of Mrs Burgess and in the light of the discussion and the available information **write a letter** to the Staff Director of Wilson-Waller Limited accepting or refusing the post offered and giving your reasons for so doing.

Task 4

For a variety of reasons which have nothing to do with her decision about the agency job, the Burgesses decide to live in or very near Telford itself, in a private house rather than in a Development Corporation one. Bearing in mind their financial circumstances – Mr Burgess is paid on the basic Burnham Scale – **devise the letter** which they would now send to local estate agents asking for information about available property.

Assignment 4D – Setting up shop

For the purpose of this assignment we should suppose that Mrs Burgess has accepted the post and has decided to set up a small office from which to operate the agency. She finds suitable premises consisting of an office of modern design roughly 4 metres × 5 metres in size with a small anteroom. The premises have previously been rented by a market research organisation which has wound up its work in the area and left, but the telephone, although cut off, is still in place with an extension in each room.

Task 1

Write the text of a letter to the local Telephone Manager asking to be allowed to take over the telephone line, giving a date from which you are prepared to be responsible for the charges, and requesting that the extension in the outer office be removed.

Task 2

The premises are to be set up with a small waiting room in the outer office and a working office in the inner one. The latter has windows running the length of one of the longer sides. In small groups, **work out what furniture the office would require,** and assess the cost of equipping it (a) with new furniture from a trade catalogue (on which Wilson-Waller would secure a 20% discount) and (b) with good second-hand office furniture purchased from a local supplier or dealer.

Task 3

Prepare the text of a circular letter to the part-time agents in the area covered by the new office informing them of the setting up of the office and enclosing the text of the company's standard circular memorandum to part-time agents about their relationships with the local full-time agent. Set out briefly the nature of your background and experience with the firm and your knowledge of agency work, and invite the agents in the area to call and see you in the course of the first month after the office opens.

Task 4

Discuss how Mrs Burgess should deal with the following letter which arrives without an address and unsigned:

"Dear Madam,

I saw in the new Wilson-Waller catalogue that your now the area agent here and I have to make a complaint. Theres an agent living in this road who pesters the life out of all of us trying to get us to buy things from the catalogue. She has nice coffee parties for the women folk around here and then when everyone is nice and friendly brings out her catalogue and does her sales pitch. Its making a lot of bad feeling in the road and you ought really to stop her. Her name is Wendy Walker and I hate having to do this to her.

Yours sincerely"

Assignments Group 5
Family in action

Reginald Charnwood is a Foreman Electrician aged 50. He was in charge of electrical maintenance work at a group of factories in the central area of Oldchester for over ten years, and 2½ years ago took a new job with the same firm, commissioning and maintaining the electrical side at a new factory where the electrical equipment was particularly important. This factory is on the industrial estate at a new town fifteen miles out of the old industrial city of Oldchester. His main spare time interest apart from his allotment is the history of the Oldchester/Worsdell area, and he has recently become interested in its industrial archaeology.

Claire, his wife, trained as an infant school teacher but married after her first year of teaching. She went back to teaching when her children had reached secondary school age, and is now a Deupty Head of a large primary school in Worsdell. Her interests are in dressmaking, pottery, and the local Labour Party — not because she is very politically minded, but because she was brought up to believe in it and has never lost this belief. Joan Charnwood qualified as a nurse at the age of 21 and promptly went off to a two-year job at an eye hospital in Melbourne, Australia. She is due to return fairly soon, and at the age of 23 shows every sign of wanting to make a long and ambitious career in nursing.

Michael is a very able boy of 18. He spent many of his school holidays as a teenager working with his father in the factories, and knew more electrical engineering at the age of 15 than any of his teachers. He was good at mathematics, too, and for many years was fascinated by the stock market and business pages of the newspaper. Although he had done well at school up to the age of 16, he was thoroughly bored by the teaching, and decided to leave. Wanting to qualify as an accountant with a view to going into industrial management, he is working as an articled clerk with a firm of accountants in the centre of Oldchester. His main hobby is the collecting and repairing of old steam engines, particularly those of small size.

The family made the move to Worsdell easily and smoothly. In most respects the new town is typical of its kind, developed from the early 1960s on the basis of a former village called South Nock. By 1975 its population had reached 35,000, but the ultimate target of 90,000 by 1995 was revised recently to a target of 60,000 by 1988. The town already has a substantial shopping centre, a sports complex, a small theatre and a full provision of other community facilities.

Unlike most new towns, however, Worsdell was built on a very uneven site which is marked by a series of deep, narrow valleys. One of the early railways ran on the bluff between two of these valleys, crossing to the opposite side of one of them at the point which became the focus of the village of South Nock itself. At the time of the planning of the new town, the villagers agreed to the scheme on a number of conditions. The valley on which South Nock stood was to be preserved as a permanent open space, the village itself was to be left as unchanged as possible, and the 15-acre woodland at the site of Nockham Manor was to be maintained as a public park. The old railway has been disused for over thirty years, and the big station serving the new town is over a mile from the old line.

Assignment 5A – Understanding the picture

1. What are the differences between local history and industrial archaeology?
2. Would you find it surprising to learn that Michael shares his mother's political outlook? What evidence is there in the account given above which suggests anything about Michael's political attitudes?
3. In the course of the time you spend on this group of assignments, find out from careers literature, job advertisements, and library sources the prevailing levels of salary, expressed in terms of an annual salary, for four of the following jobs:

a. the Deputy Headship of a Group 6 Primary School which is held by Claire Charnwood.
b. the post held by Reginald Charnwood.
c. the post of Senior Nursing Officer (equivalent to Deputy Matron), which Joan Charnwood is ambitious to gain in due course.
d. a post as Chartered Accountant working as Company Treasurer to a medium-sized company, such as Michael Charnwood hopes to achieve before he is thirty.
e. the post of Chemical Process Worker in a metal refinery which is held by Reginald's younger brother, Jeff.
f. the job of Assembly Line Foreman in a furniture factory in Worsdell which is held by Jeff's son, Dick.

4. The site chosen for Worsdell is not typical of most new towns. Why have most new towns been laid out on relatively flat and open sites? What problems does a site such as that in Wordell pose for the planners or the builders?

Assignment 5B – A home for Staff Nurse Charnwood

Joan has written back from Australia to say that she has taken a job as Staff Nurse of the Eye Ward in Oldchester Infirmary, to start in four months' time. An old friend who is with her in Melbourne will be working in Oldchester Infirmary as well, and they want a house or flat to share near the hospital. The family discuss her request to find her a property, and decide that while the decision will have to be Joan's, some spade-work can be done beforehand. Because Dad's factory is expanding, and Mother is busy with a by-election, Michael agrees to do most of the work. For purposes of this assignment you should put yourself in his position. He quickly establishes that without luck or local contacts rented property is unobtainable. In any case, he knows that Joan has a nest-egg of £4,000 and the property pages of the newspapers have told him that it is cheaper to buy if one can.

Task 1

Make a collection of the house advertisement pages of local newspapers in your own area, covering several hundred houses. Study the wording of these advertisements in some detail and make a list of the technical terms used in them (e.g. integral garage, character features, in need of modernisation, rural aspect etc.). Try to establish what these terms mean: distinguish between those which are factual and those which seek to influence the client's attitudes.

Task 2

Study some further particulars issued by Estate Agents in order

1. to **compare** the further details with the newspaper advertisements where the two advertisements can be found to relate to similar houses.
2. to **draw up a short-list** of houses likely to suit the two nurses.

Task 3

Using arrangements made by your college or teacher, **obtain information** from building societies. It will be necessary to assume that the pair can put down a deposit of £4,000 and will have a joint income of £8,400 before tax. It will be necessary to check that the societies will grant mortgages on older properties, to single women, and on property which needs improvement and repair.

Task 4

Pool the findings of this investigation and **assess which houses** listed in Task 2 are most likely to qualify for a mortgage.

Task 5

Invent a thoroughly unattractive property which is nevertheless sound enough to get a mortgage, and **draw up a newspaper advertisement** for it of the kind studied previously.

Task 6

Choose a property currently advertised and known to be in unsatisfactory condition. **Draft an advertisement** for it in the style of the following, which was actually published in a Sunday paper in 1967:

```
"Run-down house:  2 decent recep., 2
bedrms, scullery, boxrm over, dirty
but dry, structure sound, could look
pretty, rabbit-patch garden, close to
railway, no car space. £4,500.
Mortgage available for improvement
buyer."
```

Task 7

Michael returns from an afternoon off with the information gained so far and finds his mother writing to Joan. 'Ah, there you are. Tell Joan how the house-hunting is going. I have left you the back flap of the airletter.' The space referred to measures 16 cm × 10 cm and your handwriting must be completely legible. **Write a progress report** which will go into that space.

Task 9

Reginald has an Aunt Mildred who lives in Oldchester and she has heard that Joan needs a flat in town. She writes to offer Joan a room in her own house. In practice this would be at least two rooms in a large house close to the Hospital with a garage and all mod. con. Unfortunately Aunt Mildred is a straight-laced widow with strong views: she will not allow alcohol in the house, will not tolerate social activities on Sundays, and likes to serve formal meals at fixed hours. Joan is a fairly conventional girl, but it would be a disaster for her to live with Aunt Mildred. **Write the letter** in which Reginald tactfully but firmly declines this offer.

Assignment 5C South Nock Viaduct

The old railway line built from Oldchester and past the valleys where Worsdell now stands was built in the 1850s and the deep valley of the River Seale was bridged by a viaduct. This structure was made of cast iron by the famous Oldchester firm of Andrew Hessletine Ltd, which went out of business in 1928 but had manufactured several oustanding pieces of ironwork in the Victorian period. The viaduct was a 3-span iron structure resting on two slender brick piers, and although the railway tracks were pulled up for scrap in 1955 the viaduct itself remained in the ownership of British Rail.

The planning agreements with the people of South Nock were reached in 1960 between the Worsdell Development Corporation, the Nounshire County Council, and Nockham Rural District Council. The latter body ceased to exist in 1974 and was absorbed into the new District Council. British Rail was not a party to these agreements, and has come to the view that, although the viaduct is still quite safe, it cannot afford the upkeep of what is now only a monument. Planning responsibilities which are not directly part of the new town do not involve the Development Corporation.

Reginald cycles through the valley below this viaduct every day on his way to work and views it with great affection. One morning, seeing a survey team at work, he stops to ask what they are doing, and learns that they are preparing the detailed plans for demolishing the viaduct. He naturally views this with some concern and realises that when the proposal becomes known there will be a considerable fuss.

Task 1

There are two local authorities involved, the Worsdell District Council and the Nounshire County Council. **Find out the basic planning responsibilities of such bodies.**

Task 2

Find out which Central Government department has responsibilities and powers in matters of this kind, and find the correct postal address of its nearest branch office.

Task 3

Find out what other public agencies or national organisations might be interested in the viaduct, and **list the secretary's name and address** for each of them.

Task 4

Write a letter to the Worsdell Evening News expressing concern, without actually asserting as fact that the demolition is to happen.

Task 5

Find out the address of the District Manager of British Rail and send him a copy of this letter, **drafting a covering note** which invites him to confirm or deny the story. This note should be careful to avoid upsetting the railway authorities.

Task 6

Working in groups, **discuss the idea that** a petition should be arranged. Decide who it should be sent to, how it should be worded, and how and where signatures should be collected.

Task 7

Devise a letter to the Chairman of the County Council and the Chairman of the District Council, drawing their attention to the terms of the agreement made with Nockham Rural District Council in 1960, and seeking their support for the preservation of the viaduct.

Task 8

The secretary of one of the national organisations consulted advises the supporters of the viaduct to brief an architect with instructions to approach the relevant Government department. The aim is to get the building listed as one of historic interest. Find out what you can about the listing of buildings as of special historical or architectural interest and **draft the letter** to the architect accordingly.

Assignment 5D – Road Safety

At the local Primary School where Claire Charnwood is Deputy Head, two children have been injured in road accidents during the term, and recently a six-year old child was killed in a road accident when returning home from school one evening. The Head Mistress has decided that special measures are necessary. The School already undertakes a large programme of routine training in the use of bicycles, which is conducted for the Education Authority by the local police Road Safety Officers. All members of the staff undertake thorough and systematic teaching of all children in the ordinary road procedures for pedestrians. The Head and Deputy have learned that one of the difficulties in the way of these programmes is the poor example which is set to children by their own parents. They decide that part of their special measures must be some kind of approach to the parents themselves.

The School Managers agreed to the use of the School Fund to produce a booklet to be circulated to parents, much of which will include special advice on taking care on the roads of the immediate locality, with some pointing to black spots and crossing points to avoid. The Head decides to use some figures to emphasise the points, and Claire is asked to find out the relevant statistics.

The Nounshire County Council Road Safety Officer provides her with the following table.

Persons Injured in road accidents during the years 1970-78 in the County

	1970	1971	1972	1973	1974	1975	1976	1977	1978
January	358	409	421	446	370	371	391	449	421
February	391	408	451	418	391	310	333	383	360
March	401	374	390	423	402	352	446	419	402
April	410	393	412	435	407	425	415	414	475
May	391	473	485	409	461	421	470	474	477
June	433	433	490	461	475	444	381	442	494
July	419	464	474	444	453	477	518	495	527
August	462	503	441	505	517	457	439	525	507
September	435	489	390	481	478	427	479	511	477
October	467	504	521	510	499	536	519	430	586
November	470	473	491	508	511	510	528	514	560
December	538	452	460	499	442	548	561	541	598

Task 1

Claire faces the problem of how to present this body of data visually in a way which most of the parents would understand. **Working in small groups, consider what visual presentations would be best** for this purpose, including among the possibilities the use of a table, a graph, a bar chart, a pie chart etc.

Task 2

Each group should decide its preferred

scheme, **should draw it in full for presentation** to the rest of the class, and be ready to explain its decision to the class.

Task 3

As part of the commentary to be included in the booklet, Claire has to write a statement about the significant features which the statistics for 1970–78 reveal. Consider whether there is a continuing annual trend, whether particular months always give better or worse figures, and whether there are possible explanations of the patterns to be seen in the figures. Then **draft the statement,** bearing in mind that it should not be more than 200 words long, and must be easy to understand for readers who may have a very low level of literacy.

Task 4

The Head and the Deputy decide to launch the leaflet at a meeting for parents which should be addressed by the County Police Road Safety Officer and, if possible, somebody very senior like the Chief Constable. They do not expect to get the Chief Constable but certainly hope that he will send his Deputy. They also hope that the meeting could include the showing of an effective Road Safety film. **Write the letter addressed to the Chief Constable** which sets out the nature of the campaign being conducted and asking for his support and, if possible, his participation. Give a number of possible dates, and include in your account of the background the basic reason why the campaign is being conducted.

Assignment 5E – Don't knock the rock

For purposes of this assignment you should assume that you are Michael Charnwood, and that you share his enthusiasm for rock music. There has been very little opportunity to see the best acts 'live' in Worsdell itself, because as yet the town has had no large concert hall, and getting tickets for them in Oldchester is not easy if you do not live in the city. However, the latest phase of the town centre development includes a multi-purpose theatre/concert hall built at considerable cost. It can seat 1,200 people and is superbly equipped, to operate as an open stage theatre, a theatre with a curtain, a concert hall or a cinema. The rock music enthusiasts in the town now feel that at last it will be possible to stage concerts by the top performers, and the Council's policy is to make the fullest possible use of the hall, catering for as wide a range of audiences as possible.

One evening, an item in the Worsdell Evening News refers to the new hall:

```
    "NEW CONCERT HALL
     VARIED PROGRAMME PLANNED

At today's meeting of the Leisure and
Amenities Committee of Worsdell District
Council, Cllr. Godfrey Millett, the Chairman,
announced plans for concerts to be held in the
new concert hall over the next year.  The
London Symphony Orchestra will give the open-
ing concert, and there will be performances by
Julian Bream, The Spinners, The Sid Lawrence
Orchestra, The Kings Singers and Oscar Peter-
son.  The Programme Sub-Committee had dis-
cussed at length whether rock music concerts
should be allowed and had decided against it.
Cllr. Millett reminded the Committee of the
damage done at a recent concert by Vic Nausea
and the Depressives at the Prince's Hall in
Oldchester and at other well-publicised
concerts by groups of this kind.  The Leisure
and Amenities Committee endorsed the prop-
osals with warm approval."
```

You are annoyed at this decision, since you feel that all rock fans are being penalized for the action of a few, by a group of

Councillors who have no understanding of the fact that rock concerts and their audiences can vary a great deal.

Task 1

Write a letter to the editor of the 'Worsdell Evening News' expressing your disappointment at the Council's decision, and asking for it to be reconsidered on the grounds that the sub-committee may not have had sufficient information.

Task 2

Write a letter to the editor of 'Melody Express', the country's leading pop music paper. You may have ideas and feelings to express in this letter which are very similar to those expressed to the local paper, but the style and approach will need to be varied considerably.

Task 3

The local paper publishes your letter, and the local radio station makes contact with you by telephone. BBC Radio Oldchester ask you to appear on a local early-evening news programme with Councillor Millett for a discussion of the issue. Consider what questions are likely to be asked, and **work out what arguments you would use.** Remember that in programmes of this kind each party to a discussion is likely to have less than $1\frac{1}{2}$ minutes in which to make its main statement, and to spend any of this time on expressing feeling rather than putting forward a reasoned argument is a waste of an opportunity.

Task 4

The Radio programme leads to a great deal of support amongst many young people, and there are protests to Councillors and others for some time, but the Committee refuses to change its position. The protests have brought together a group of Michael's age and outlook who decide to set to work to bring about a change in the rule. **Work out in discussion and summarise in note form** a strategy which such a group might adopt.

Assignments Group 6
Butley Housing Department

You are Terry Baxter, aged 17½, and are employed as a Clerk in the Housing Department of the Butley District Council. You have worked there for over a year and have shown yourself capable of handling many routine matters properly. The Housing Manager, Mr Kenneth Archer, goes through his morning mail and frequently passes items to you for reply. Sometimes he passes documents to you to deal with as you see fit. The documents which make up this group of assignments are the contents of your in-tray on a particular morning. The letters with handwritten comments have come from Mr Archer, while others have come to you direct. You will find the letters on the next page.

Assignment 6A – The Old People's Gardens

Task 1

> 54 Dove Street,
> Beetley,
> 10th May.
>
> Dear Sir,
> I am now 72 and have lived here for five years. I couldn't look after the garden when I came, and it is now growing wild. It upsets me to see this and my neighbour Mr. Rushden at No. 52 says he would like it as an allotment. This would help a lot and the rent would help my pension. I would like to ask permission to rent out my garden to Mr Rushden.
>
> Yours faithfully
> Emily Johnson
> (Mrs)

No rule against it. Seems a good idea but any payment shd. be a private affair. Reply and sign for me please. KA

Carry out Mr Archer's instruction

Task 2

```
MEMORANDUM   From: Rent Collector 5
             To:   H.O.
             Re:   22 Dove Street O.P.
                   Bungalow.
```

Mrs. Ward is vacating – one of our very best tenants. She made particular point of asking if new tenant could be someone unable or unwilling to cope with the garden, as a Percy Dawe, 17 Wren Street, uses Mrs. Ward's garden and supplies all the neighbouring O.A.P.s from it. Dawe is anxious too, and if we can oblige it would be nice to reassure him.

T.R.M.

T.B. Pl. do so, but keep it unofficial. KA.

Write an appropriate note to Mr Dawe on the basis that the Department is very likely to replace Mrs Ward with another old lady, but cannot promise to do so.

Assignment 6B – The telephone message

Task 1

Discuss in some detail what is wrong with this message.

~~Terry~~

> Terry – Please ring Jane Smith. Wants to no about housing alocation for newly married cauples or something. Maggie.

Task 2

Jane Smith telephones again, and Terry Baxter is not available. Margaret Walker takes the call and must explain that Terry is out and take an adequate message. **Simulate the conversation.**

Assignment 6C – Demolition area

> 72, Underwood Road,
> Butley.
>
> Sir,
>   This house has been bought by the Council because all the terraces around here are being knocked down. We're supposed to be at the top of the list for new Council houses but we've been waiting two years since you bought the house. The windows and doors are warped so none of them will shut properly. We wake up at night and my wife and daughter are afraid of burglars. The fence and gate have been knocked down by vandals and the toilet doesn't work properly any more — yesterday the door fell off.
>   The house isn't fit to live in and I would like to know what you are going to do about it.
>   Yours sincerely,
>   R. Nelson
>
> *Hard to make out in full. Can you do better? Nelson bad payer of rent but has a point. Tell him demolition scheduled for Sept. He will get 4 wks notice of new housing. If you have other suggestions please arrange them. KA*

Task 1

Write the letter to Mr Nelson requested by Mr Archer.

Task 2

You know that Roger Normanton, 5th Year Tutor at Stockbridge Comprehensive School, runs a superbly organised Youth Aid Scheme. This seems a very good case for referring to him, but you have to alert Normanton to the possibility that the family may be difficult. **Write a suitable confidential memorandum.** You can assume that Normanton is used to receiving such notes, and is thoughtful and careful about how much he passes on to his 5th year pupils.

Assignment 6D – The meeting arrangements

> Association of Housing Managers
> Central District
>
> Hon Sec:
> F. C. Clements,
> The Gazebo,
> Western Overdale,
> Oakland,
> Trent.
>
> 9th May, 19--
>
> Dear Jack,
>   Could I remind you that at the A.G.M. you kindly offered to hold the Summer Quarter meeting of the Association at Butley. We should have an interesting discussion, as Dixon wants to raise the Green Paper proposals, which he is almost alone among us in supporting.
>
>   If you could confirm that we can come to Butley at, say, 2.00 p.m. on June 29th, I can let the members know in the newsletter next week.
>
>   Yours sincerely,
>   Frank.
>   Frank Clements
>
> *T.B. Let him know that this is OK, but 2-30: the Committee Room is booked until 2-15 for some farewell party. Let Ethel know about coffee and biscuits for 3, and tell Frank to instruct members to use car park to left of main gate, not the Councillors one to the right.   for me to sign   KA.*

Task 1

Draft Mr Archer's reply to Mr Clements in a suitable format, for Mr Archer to sign.

Task 2

Write a memo for Ethel (Mrs Williams, the Canteen Manageress, who is a good friend of Mr Archer but seems to you rather formidable) asking for the coffee to be supplied to the Committee Room.

Assignment 6E – Councillor Hunt's constituent

                              64 Mafeking Road,
                              Butley. BU3 8dW.
                              10th May, 19 --

Housing Manager,
Butley District Council,
Butley, BU3 5NB

Dear Mr. Archer

    Mrs. Margaret Small, 15 Crown
    Avenue, Butley

    Mrs. Small is one of my constituents, and has complained to me that she has not been allocated an old person's bungalow. She is 75, a widow and suffers from arthritis. She can walk quite well and cooks and cleans for herself, but she finds it difficult to manage the stairs and impossible to maintain her garden.

    XXXXXXXXXXX Mrs. Small /tells me she/ has applied for a warden-supervised bungalow in Butley before, and over a year ago one of your officers visited her. Since then, three bungalows have fallen vacant, and have been allocated to people who are in my judgement less deserving than Mrs Small.

    It would appear that your offices are being less than fair in allocating these bungalows, and I intend to raise the matter at the next meeting of the Housing Committee. However, I thought it only fair to let you know of this in advance.

               Yours sincerely,

               David Hunt (Cllr)

T.B. Dig out what you can on this and let me have a summary a.s.a.p. KA

You check the file of application letters and can find only one, dated February 16th of the previous year. During May last year she was visited by a housing officer and his report reads:

    Mrs. Small, 15 Crown Avenue.
    This lady suffers from arthritis but
    is otherwise in good health and quite
    capable of looking after herself.
    The accommodation is good and quite
    close to several relatives. Her
    daughter-in-law is pressing for a
    protected bungalow but Mrs. Small is
    perfectly happy where she is. The
    daughter-in-law makes much more of the
    stairs problem than she does. Her
    house is a 3-bedroom family house,
    which we could well use, but super-
    vised bungalows are in much shorter
    supply and Mrs. Small does not really
    have a case for one.

Terry searches the file to discover the allocation of the three bungalows referred to by Mr Hunt. One went to a lady with a good case who had been waiting three years; one was given to a couple younger than Mrs Small but rendered homeless by a Compulsory Purchase Order; the third went to a gentleman crippled after a stroke. The number of people over seventy on the waiting list for housing is twenty-two, and four of them are marked on the file as in 'urgent need of supervised accommodation'.

Task 1

Summarise for Mr Archer the important facts of this case.

Task 2

Mr Archer asks you to accompany him to a meeting of the Housing Committee and Mrs Small's case is about to come up when he is called away. You have to explain the Department's decisions. **Present orally the case you would make.**

Task 3

After the meeting it is necessary to place on file a short Note for File recording the case made to the Committee, and the Committee's reception of it. **Write this note.**

Assignment 6F – The housing conference

For purposes of this task, you should assume that Waterton is a large city which can be reached by a main line train within an hour, and that the place where the Conference is held is within walking distance of the station. **Then carry out Mr Archer's instructions.**

May 12

Terry – You will have seen the papers about the conference for Housing Officers and Councillors in Waterton on June 4 about Housing Administration. The Chairman of the Housing Committee (Cllr. Mrs McKean), Cllrs. Forebush and Hunt wish to attend this and wish me to join them. Would you look up the trains to see whether we can get there for a meeting starting at 10-30 and finishing at 16-30, and get back at a reasonable time. Would you also work out whether it would in practice be cheaper for us all to travel in my car. Then set up a letter for me to send to the three Cllrs. confirming the arrangement